MORE STORIES FROM MY FATHER'S COURT

MORE STORIES FROM MY FATHER'S COURT

ঙ৯৯

ISAAC BASHEVIS SINGER

ঙ৯৯

TRANSLATED FROM THE YIDDISH BY

CURT LEVIANT

FARRAR, STRAUS AND GIROUX

NEW YORK

Farrar, Straus and Giroux
19 Union Square West, New York 10003

Copyright © 1956, 1997 by Israel Zamir
Translation copyright © 2000 by Curt Leviant
All rights reserved
Distributed in Canada by Douglas & McIntyre Ltd.
Printed in the United States of America
Designed by Jonathan D. Lippincott
First edition, 2000

Library of Congress Cataloging-in-Publication Data
Singer, Isaac Bashevis, 1904–
[Essays. English. Selections]
More stories from my father's court / by Isaac Bashevis Singer ;
translated by Curt Leviant.
p.   cm.
ISBN 0-374-21343-7 (alk. paper)
1. Singer, Isaac Bashevis, 1904–Childhood and youth.   2. Rabbinical
courts—Poland—Warsaw.   3. Singer, Isaac Bashevis, 1904–
Translations into English.   I. Title
PJ5129.S49 A25 2000   00-037583
839'.143—dc21

The stories in this collection first appeared as newspaper columns in Yiddish
in *The Jewish Daily Forward* between the years 1955 and 1960.

CONTENTS

∽∾

CONTENTS

MORE STORIES FROM MY FATHER'S COURT

CHAIM THE LOCKSMITH

 හ

Although everyone called him Chaim the locksmith, he was actually what we here in America call a plumber. He repaired water pipes, especially clogged toilet lines, a frequent problem in our street.

Chaim was a man of middling height, strong and broad-shouldered, with a face brown as bronze and a beard to match. His clothes seemed to be dusted with rust. Although he was still young, his face had the lines and wrinkles of a laboring man who does not spare himself. Summer and winter he wore a short jacket and high boots. He always carried pipes, hammers, files, pliers, and odd pieces of iron. Even his voice had a metallic twang. On Sabbath, Chaim the locksmith prayed in our apartment and ate the Third Sabbath Meal with us. Sometimes, while drinking a tumbler of brandy, he would shake my hand. His hand was hard as iron.

Aside from fixing toilets, Chaim was summoned wherever there was trouble: a fire, a collapsed ceiling, a stuck door, a broken oven. He was the only one who didn't mind getting smeared with ashes and soot. He burdened himself with other onerous tasks as well. In addition to being part of the group that prayed in our apartment, Chaim belonged to the Sleepover Volunteers, whose members would spend nights with the sick. After a hard day's work, Chaim was sent to care for people suffering from typhus or delirium who needed the help of a strong man. God had blessed Chaim with strength, and with it he served God. When people begged Chaim not to exhaust himself, he would shrug his shoulders and reply, "If you're given broad shoulders, you must bear the burden."

Chaim the locksmith had a few daughters; his youngest child was a boy about nine or ten years older than I, named Zanvel. Chaim's love for his only son was boundless. I never heard him speak of anything but the boy: Zanvel can already read syllables, Zanvel has just started the Five Books of Moses, Zanvel has begun studying Gemara. Chaim had already decided that Zanvel must be a scholar and become a rabbi. Whenever Chaim visited us he would say, "My Zanvele will be a rabbi."

"God willing," Father replied.

"I just want to live to see one thing—my Zanvele deciding rabbinic questions."

This wasn't merely a wish; it was the only hope on which Chaim the locksmith's efforts were focused. He sent Zanvel to study with the best teachers; early on, he dressed him in Hasidic clothing. Chaim paid a young Hasid to watch over him, study with him, and discuss Torah and Hasidic rebbes with him. Zanvel displayed a love of learning; yet with his fair skin, blue eyes, and blond sidecurls, he resembled his mother, not his father. With his thin, high-pitched voice, it was hard to believe that he was Chaim's son.

Chaim brought Zanvel to Father for an oral examination each Sabbath. Mother would offer him fruit, and as Zanvel sat with us, wearing a cap and a belted satin gaberdine, Father would discuss Hasidic matters with him. A bit farther away sat the locksmith, his face shining with an otherworldly joy. His bronzed face seemed to melt with pleasure, and the eyes beneath his bushy brows were filled with light. Perhaps such was the happiness of the Jews at Mount Sinai when God revealed Himself amid fire.

When Chaim's wife complained that he paid scant attention to his daughters, he would defend himself by saying, Don't I love the girls? He loved them more than his own life. But after all, girls cannot study Torah. They run around in the courtyard and are interested only in clothing, trifles, and nonsense. How could Chaim compare the joy the girls gave him with that of Zanvel? Zanvel sat over a Talmud and his little voice echoed throughout the courtyard. In the study house respectable Jews came and discussed a bit of Gemara with him. One hundred years from now Zanvel would recite the Kaddish after Chaim's death. And what's more, Zanvel was weak and gentle, a silken lad. The girls resembled him, Chaim.

Indeed, it was true. The girls had brown faces, thick braids, high chests. They sang plaintive songs about the *Titanic* and about various love affairs. On Sabbaths they cracked pumpkin seeds at the gate of the apartment house and secretly went to the movies. So how could they be compared to little Zanvel?

Just yesterday Zanvel was a cheder lad—and now he was already on the threshold of young adulthood. He studied Torah with my father and attended Talmud lectures given by some head of a yeshiva. He was awarded a nickel-plated watch for his mastery of fifty pages of Talmud. This was the time when yeshiva students strayed from the straight and narrow path, reading newspapers and perusing forbidden secular books. In our house we feared for Zanvel. Everyone knew that if Zanvel stumbled, the heart of that strong Jew, Chaim the locksmith, would burst like an overfilled balloon. Chaim would have been able to withstand any blow, except a tragedy involving Zanvel.

But, thank God, Zanvel did not go down the crooked path. He craved studying, swayed during prayers, and in time also went to see a Hasidic rebbe. One day, Chaim the locksmith came to us and declared, "My Zanvel is in Gur . . . at the rebbe's court."

And he humbly bent his head as if silently wondering, Why am I worthy of such joy? Do I deserve it? It's unbelievable . . . incredible!

When the First World War began and Zanvel had to report to the draft board, it was a catastrophe for Chaim the locksmith. If Zanvel was sent to the barracks and to the front, all his plans would be ruined. Chaim wandered around distraught, his face no longer brown but black as a chimney sweep's. Some suggested that Zanvel should injure himself just enough to make him unfit for military service. But Chaim couldn't bear the idea that Zanvel would somehow be disfigured. In his mind Zanvel was like a Temple sacrifice which had to be absolutely without blemish.

After a while Chaim the locksmith decided to place Zanvel in hiding instead. He found a garret where Zanvel sat and studied for days on end. He did not set foot on the street, lest he be asked for identity papers. Chaim the locksmith himself watched out for an inspector who might enter the courtyard. Chaim was careful, his wife was careful, his daughters were careful. The entire courtyard was on the alert. In the meantime, Zanvel sat surrounded by books and studied. He drank tea, swayed, hummed some melody, and ate the food his mother brought him.

Then Warsaw was beset by inflation and Chaim the locksmith had little work. The poor people of the neighborhood could no longer afford to have their toilets fixed. But Chaim's meager income provided soups and grits and fresh little rolls for his little Zanvel. For under no circumstances should a young man sitting in a prisonlike setting and studying Torah suffer any want.

When the Germans entered Warsaw, Zanvel no longer had to hide from the gentile authorities. He was free to come and go as he pleased, and Chaim the locksmith made a banquet. By now Zanvel had a little blond beard; he had straightened up, developed a long neck, sunken cheeks, and a pointy Adam's apple, which bobbed up and down his throat. He already spoke with a rabbinic intonation. Many pious Jews and religious functionaries gathered at the banquet—which ruined Chaim the locksmith. He had no income of his own, and he had to sell, pawn, and deprive himself and his daughters of their last bite of food. At this banquet Zanvel delivered a quibbling, hair-splitting discourse and debated some recondite Talmudic points with the scholars present. Chaim the locksmith laughed and cried.

Chaim began to look bad. First of all, he didn't have enough to eat. Second, his daughters, who had started down a slippery slope, caused him anguish. And finally, the fear that something might happen to Zanvel finished him off. Chaim coughed and his back bent over as if under a heavy burden. He was urged to see a doctor, to get some fresh air in the countryside. But Chaim the locksmith just laughed.

"What else should I do? Eat marzipan candy?"

A match was soon arranged for Zanvel; the bride-to-be was a rabbi's daughter. The bride's family was usually responsible for the dowry, but when a rabbi agrees to a match with a locksmith, *he* wants to be paid. Chaim had no money but promised a dowry, so when the Germans began building a railroad nearby and he heard they needed locksmiths, mechanics, and metal workers, Chaim the locksmith went off to work for the Germans.

His wife came to us crying that Chaim was killing himself. He labored outside in the freezing cold, in snowstorms and downpours. Workers were dropping like flies. Chaim was doing the work of three men. When he managed to come home for a day, his appearance frightened his family. He was no longer brown or black—but yellow. White hairs threaded his beard. His voice was hoarse and he coughed like a consumptive.

My father warned Chaim that it is forbidden to sacrifice oneself for the sake of some dowry or prestigious lineage, and that one's life and well-being take precedence over everything else. Father took a volume of the *Code of Law* from a bookshelf and showed Chaim that when a pregnant woman is about to give birth, everyone is permitted to violate the Sabbath for her, even though one person would suffice. Such is the value that the Torah places on a human life. But Chaim the locksmith answered, "Rabbi, the devil won't take me."

Zanvel became engaged, and the party cost plenty of German marks. Once Zanvel married, Chaim again spent a fortune. Then came the good news: Zanvel had been offered a rabbinic position in a small shtetl.

That would be the last time Chaim visited our apartment. He came in, positioned himself in the doorway, and began to sing like someone in a Purim costume: "Mazel tov! Zanvel is a rabbi!" he called out, and then began to cry. He seized Father's hand and kissed it.

"Zanvel may be a rabbi, but you're killing yourself," Mother said ominously.

Chaim gave out a sickly laugh. "How can it hurt? My Zanvel is a rabbi." Chaim attempted a little dance, but his feet were swollen and he managed only one small hop before he had to sit down.

After this, Chaim the locksmith took to his bed and was prepared to die. The man had overworked himself, taxed his strength beyond measure. To those who paid him a sick call he declared, "I just barely managed to raise him . . . now I'm ready . . ."

The son came to visit his father, and the courtyard grew black with people. Zanvel had long sidecurls and wore a long black rabbinic coat, a silk jacket, shoes and socks. As Zanvel sat down beside his father, Chaim the locksmith gave him the smile of a mortally ill man and asked, "Zanvele, you'll say Kaddish for me?"

"Father, you'll get well."

"Why should I get well? I've accomplished all that I wanted to do." And then Chaim the locksmith cracked a locksmith joke: "What more can I do? Fix a few more toilets?"

9

Chaim the locksmith died and was given a big funeral. The son eulogized his father at the gravesite. Following the wagon were rabbis, synagogue trustees, respectable Jews. But my father was angry at Chaim. He maintained that one should not sacrifice himself even for the sake of Torah.

"A low-class man remains a low-class man," Father said bitterly. For days on end he walked about upset. Then one morning he remarked, "I think I saw Chaim the locksmith. He was shining like the sun."

"Did he say anything to you?"

"He told me where he lives in the Garden of Eden."

"Where?"

Father whispered the secret into Mother's ear. Mother turned white. It was hard to believe that Chaim the locksmith could achieve such heights. But on the other hand, he had given his life for the sake of the Torah. Hadn't Rabbi Akiva done the same?

THE *SHOCHET*'S WIFE

ぺつ

Husband and wife came—separately—into our apartment and at once began bad-mouthing each other. She was young but wore an old-fashioned woman's cap and had an old face, teary eyes, and a reddish nose. She blew her nose into her handkerchief and complained to my mother.

"He's a sadist, a murderer. He's not a human being but a killer."

"What does he do to you?"

"He sucks my blood."

"For example?"

"I can't describe it. He sucks his fill of me like a leech. He's only good to me when he wants me."

The young woman whispered something into Mother's ear. Mother nodded, a sign that such is a woman's lot in life.

"Rebbetzin, he sucks the life out of me and for no good reason. I want to run away. But where would I run to? When parents give their daughter away, they no longer want to see her again. We had a goy in the house who used to say, 'When you throw out garbage, you don't want it back.'"

11

"A person isn't garbage," Mother said resolutely.

"When you have five daughters you want to send them away and hear good news from them—from far off. My mother is a fine woman, but she can also be so cutting that you feel it in your gut. Here I'm mistress of my own household."

"You're right. One mustn't rush into such things," Mother agreed. "Sometimes a person behaves terribly, then suddenly becomes good. Men don't articulate what troubles them. They hold everything in."

"He comes here to see you. What does he say?" the woman asked.

"He doesn't say anything bad, God forbid."

"Still, what does he say?"

"He complains about other people—not about you."

"That's here. But at home I'm the sacrificial chick. It's my fault they didn't appoint him a licensed city *shochet.* He walks around with the slaughtering knife in hand and sometimes I get the feeling he wants to slaughter me, God forbid."

Mother shuddered. "Pardon me, but you're talking nonsense."

"I'm afraid of him. All he does is sharpen his knives and test them on his fingernail. He's no saint, Rebbetzin. He trims his beard."

Mother's face paled. "What are you talking about?"

"How else would he get that rounded little beard?" the woman informed on him. "He cuts it. He cuts it. He eats before morning prayers, too."

Mother began adjusting her wig. "I don't want to hear any more."

"Rebbetzin, he came to me during my unclean days."

Mother threw an angry glance at me. "Why are you standing here? Go back to your books. Don't hang around the house all day like an old granny."

I went down to the courtyard and pondered: What are "unclean days"? And what's the meaning of "he came to me"? Since they live together, he's always with her anyway. Grownups have such bizarre secrets.

A couple of days later, Wolf the slaughterer came to our apartment. He was a man of average height, rather chubby, with a rounded beard, red cheeks, and bulging, baggy eyes. His glance was hard and cold, like that of a dead fish. He rolled his *r*'s, and words came out of his mouth and thick lips like little stones.

"Things are no good. They're bad. Awful. First the precinct captain comes and then the cop. And each one's palm has to be greased. If not, I can't work. If you slaughter without a permit, you get three months in jail. The goose dealers know this and they make a fool of me. They pay me half the fee they offer the licensed city slaughterers. They're roughnecks who have no respect for anyone. The worst riffraff in Warsaw! They fiddle away a few hours and pocket fifty rubles a week while I slave well into the night and barely cover my expenses. I find it hard to buy clothes. Working in the cellar is ruining my eyes. And to top it off, my wife is a spendthrift. All she does is buy buy buy and throw money around. People assume that slaughterers roll in money, but I'm still a debtor."

Father listened while perusing a holy book. He had no patience for that piddling *shochet* or his stories. Nevertheless, when a Jew comes in, he can't be thrown out, God forbid.

Mother also sat at the table. "A woman has a better feel for what's needed in a house than a man," she said. "It's best when a man doesn't interfere with the running of a household."

"If I didn't she'd spend our last penny. Normal women shop when they need something. But she buys just like that. It's a kind of madness. We have enough meat in the house. A *shochet* never lacks for meat. I get chickens, geese, ducks, even a turkey for Pesach. Why do we need beef if we can eat chicken every day? But still she runs to the butcher shop every single day and buys a piece of beef, kishka, and who knows what else! If only she'd eat it. But she just sniffs it and puts it aside, which is bearable during the winter; but meat spoils in summer and starts to smell . . . and that causes the worst illnesses."

I too listened, and concluded that both sides were right. But I didn't understand why he comes to her during her unclean days, I nearly asked, but I kept silent.

For a while no one spoke. The wick in the lamp sucked the kerosene. Then Wolf the *shochet* said, "I've been advised to go to America." He pronounced "America" with a hard rolled *r*.

"To America, of all places?"

"Slaughterers make a fortune over there."

"In America one cannot be a Jew," said Father.

"They're Jews, they're Jews," Wolf the *shochet* replied. "A *shochet* there is also a *mohel*, a profession that makes one rich. I once knew a little *shochet*, a perfect shlimazel, a clumsy oaf. He once slaughtered a rooster, and even though its throat was slit, it ran around and crowed. It even leaned over and ate."

The colors in Mother's face changed. "Don't tell us such stories!"

"But it's the truth. The shlimazel didn't make the incision in the proper place. He couldn't work as a slaughterer after that, so he went off to America. In New York he became a rich man. There a *shochet* doesn't even wear a beard."

"They shave off their beards?" Father cried out.

"They say it's done with some kind of powder. We got a photograph of him and he's standing there with a naked face, looking like a dandy from Marshalkovska Street. I couldn't recognize him at all. He also divorced his wife and married a New York girl."

"And what happened to the first wife?" Mother asked.

"Who knows?"

My tongue itched. I wanted to call out, You cut your beard, too! But I restrained myself with all my might.

Then Father said, "What does all this come down to? We don't live forever and ultimately we'll have to give an accounting. People don't live forever in America either."

"No, but as long as one lives, one really lives!" Wolf the *shochet* maintained. "A *shochet* there is like a municipal scribe here. He puts in his couple of hours and then is free to do what he wants. The *shochtim* there wear modern clothes like Frenchmen or Germans, and take strolls in the park with their wives. And when they slaughter they wear white aprons."

"But who inspects their slaughtering knives?"

"Who needs inspections? The *shochet* himself knows the law. And if he doesn't know it, then too bad. In America a *shochet* does not study *Tevuos Shor*. He just looks through a little rule book or studies the *Yoreh De'ah* and the *Be'er Hetev*. And it goes without saying that he doesn't consult the *Pri Megadim** either. The main thing over there is to do everything quickly. The goyim kill their animals with a machine . . ."

"Enough!"

The *shochet* left. A couple of days later his wife returned. "Rebbetzin, I can't take it anymore."

She didn't yell and didn't cry but hissed like a goose, spat like a snake. She put a finger to her throat signaling how high the water had risen.

"What is it now?" Mother asked.

"Rebbetzin, he wants to go to America. What should I do? How can I go there? Either he's crazy—may it happen to my enemies!—or he's a heretic. There's a dybbuk in him, no doubt about it, an evil spirit. What should I do? To whom should I go? Warsaw is such a big city."

"Does he want to go alone?"

"You think I'm going to go to America with him? Warsaw isn't *trayf* enough? I need America? Jews there work on the Sabbath, woe unto us! People walk upside down there, head on the ground, feet in the air. Everyone talks English and only the devil understands them. I'm not going to America."

"And he really wants to go?"

"Rebbetzin, if he says he'll go, he'll go. Every other day another crazy notion takes hold of him. Now he wants to buy a gramophone, where music comes out of a huge trumpet. I tell

---

**Tevuos Shor*, a widely used text containing laws pertaining to ritual slaughtering. *Yoreh De'ah*, the section of the *Code of Law* that deals with ritual slaughtering. The *Be'er Hetev* and *Pri Megadim*, commentaries to the *Code of Law* generally included in that text. (Author)

him, Where in the world did you ever hear that a *shochet* should have something like that? That's more appropriate for beardless musicians. But it's like talking to the wall. He wants to give in to conversion. Rebbetzin, the truth is—he wants a new wife!"

The *shochet*'s wife began to sob and blow her nose into her handkerchief with a harsh, grating sound. "What am I supposed to do?"

"Does he want a divorce?" Mother asked.

"Why shouldn't he? He's got a hankering for a young one. He wants a loose girl, a bareheaded piece who doesn't keep Yiddishkeit. In America a *shochet*'s wife walks around with uncovered, messy hair and they go the the theater together . . . Who knows if they have a ritual bath over there? It's a topsy-turvy world over there, and that's where he wants to run off to and leave me here a deserted wife . . . So tell me what should I do?"

"Let him give you money."

"He says he doesn't have any money. And if he does, I don't know where he keeps it. He cries he's in debt. How much do we need? We're only two. He slaughters all day long. He makes a living, he does. He puts money away, but if I buy half a pound of meat because chickens are coming out of my nose, he starts raving and ranting. Rebbetzin, it's not right to say so, but I don't want to eat the fowl that he's slaughtered. He's corrupt. I want glatt kosher meat under the strictest supervision. My grandfather, may he rest in peace, fasted every Monday and Thursday. When he died they put a Talmud folio on his stretcher. My grandmother, may she rest in peace, was a saintly, upstanding woman. In our house, three days before Pesach they kashered the stove till it glowed. We didn't even eat knaydls until the last day of the holiday. In America he'll become completely wild. If he trims his beard here, what will he do there?"

"This is not a good situation," Mother said.

"Should I divorce him?"

"It's certainly better than remaining an *agunah*, a deserted wife."

The *shochet*'s wife left. We heard her crying on the stairwell. I went out into the courtyard, and of their own accord my feet led me to the dark cellar where Wolf was slaughtering. At first I couldn't see a thing, but soon my eyes grew accustomed to the darkness. The cellar was full of blood and feathers and stacked cages filled with live fowl. Wolf stood working next to a washtub brimming with blood. He seized a chicken forcefully and, it seemed to me, with anger. He turned its head back, flicked out a little feather, made a cut, and threw the chicken to a girl in a bloody jacket who plucked feathers. She had a big bosom, thick hands, a broad neck, red cheeks, and eyes as black as cherries. Sitting on a kind of shoemaker's bench, she plucked with a murderous fury while the bird was still quivering and thrashing about.

I watched open-mouthed. A moment ago the bird had been alive and a minute later all its feathers were gone. The other birds stuck their heads out of the cages, looked around, clucked, and closed their red lids. How could God see all this and remain silent? I asked myself. Why did He need such a world? Why did He create all this? And who would repay all these little chickens for their suffering? I was angry at Wolf the *shochet* for committing these murders. I recalled that he came to his wife during her unclean days and felt nauseous.

A couple of months later Wolf divorced his wife and gave her several hundred rubles. Even before he left for America, he began wearing Western dress in Warsaw, parading around the courtyard in a short jacket, long trousers, and polished boots. From the vest covering his fat paunch dangled the chain of a pocket watch. Word had spread that Wolf was having a love affair with the feather plucker and planned on taking her to America. My mother went to the window and gazed down at the transformed Wolf the *shochet*, who had abandoned all shame. She wanted Father to come to the window, too, but he said, "What for? It's a waste of time."

Father brought the holy book he was studying closer to him, as if to hide his face from the world and from its lusts and temptations.

A year passed. The *shochet* went off to America. His wife moved out of our courtyard. Then one day she sent regards through a neighbor of ours who told us that the *shochet*'s ex-wife had married a crude and common young butcher. She no longer wore her old-fashioned cap but had donned a curled marriage wig. She stood by the butcher block in a white apron like a born butcher's wife. My mother listened to our neighbor in silence. A sadness radiated from her pale eyes.

"*Nu*, that's how human beings are," she observed.

A GUEST IN THE *SHTIBL*

ယင

One afternoon a gigantic, broad-shouldered man with a ruddy face, blond beard, and wild eyes entered the *shtibl*, the small Hasidic prayer room, for the Mincha service. His garb was neither long nor short. He wore a fur cape and a hooded caftan that looked as though it had been made in the Middle Ages. His boots had broad uppers into which he had tucked his baggy trousers. He removed a tiny siddur from his pocket and began reciting the Order of Sacrifices.

He prayed with great devotion, but the words he uttered were hard and heavy as stones. People watched him and shrugged. "Who is that?" they asked.

After prayers the worshippers greeted him with *"Sholom aleichem"* and asked where he was from.

"Oh, from far away."

"From where?"

"Russia."

"Which town?"

He named one the Warsaw Hasidim had never heard of.

"And what's your name?"

"Avraham."

The way he pronounced "Avraham" made them realize he wasn't a Jew like other Jews. After several exchanges they discovered that Avraham was a convert. He was a peasant from a remote Russian province who had come to live on this Jewish street in Warsaw, where he was now a tinsmith.

When asked why he had become a Jew, he cried out, "Because the Jews have the truth!"

The Jews were amazed. They were even more amazed that he had come to pray in a Hasidic *shtibl* rather than a regular *shul*, but everyone was welcoming and friendly to him. When he was called to the Torah for an *aliyah*—summoned as "Reb Avraham ben Avraham"—the convert touched the Torah with the *tzitzis* of his tallis, kissed it, and recited the blessing in a deep bass voice that seemed to come from a barrel or a tomb. The younger boys giggled and pinched one another. The Torah reader just managed to contain his laughter by swaying and frowning. Yes, here before us was a Jew, a pious Jew—in the shape and form of a goy.

Before long the convert began causing trouble. Hasidim habitually talk during prayers, but when the convert heard someone chatting, he turned red and then pale with anger and yelled: "*Nu*—shh!"

And put a finger to his lips.

During the Silent Devotion he stood immersed in prayer for a long time. The prayer leader hadn't the patience to wait for him to conclude and began the repetition of the Silent Devotion. This caused the convert to miss the Kedusha, which angered him.

"You're rushing through the prayers," he complained. "You're forgetting that you're speaking to God."

The convert had apparently studied the holy texts and knew the laws, for he asked, "Do you count money so quickly, too? One has to pray like one counts money."

The Hasidim conceded that the convert was right, but Hasidim are still not Misnagdim.* They would apologize to the convert and admit that he was right, but the next day the scene repeated itself. The convert yelled, pounded the table with his heavy fist, and shouted that the Messiah wasn't coming because the Jews were sinning.

But the boys had even more problems with him. They all talked during prayers, ran around, pinched one another, and snickered. The convert raised the roof. What annoyed him most was that the youngsters did not say "Blessed be He and blessed be His name" and "Amen" at the proper places. His own resonant "Blessed be He and blessed be His name" and "Amen" shook the walls. His goyish piety awakened in the boys and even in the grownups an irresistible desire to laugh. Even the chazan himself had to laugh into his fist in the middle of his prayers.

On Yom Kippur the convert did something wild: instead of wearing socks, he stood barefoot. His feet were gigantic and his unusually wide big toes were topped by misshapen toenails. A mere glance at those feet and one couldn't help laughing. On Yom Kippur night, during the cantor's Kol Nidrei, the entire congregation was in a paroxysm of laughter. They beat their

*The opponents of Hasidim.

chests during the "For our sins" prayer and chuckled into their High Holiday prayer books.

The convert stood with a tallis wrapped over his white linen robe. When he pounded his chest, it echoed throughout the sanctuary, as did his pitiful weeping. His form stood out from all the other tallises and linen robes. He wore a gilded yarmulke that made him look not like a Jew but like one of the saints the gentiles paint on church walls. The Hasidim concluded that they would have to rid themselves of this Ivan—but how? Can Jews drive away a goy who has taken upon himself the yoke of Yiddishkeit? Wasn't he a tzaddik, a saintly man?

After the Evening Service the convert did not go home. Instead, he spent the night in the *shtibl.* All night long he recited psalms. The next morning, before the Torah was taken out of the Ark, the convert made a scene. The trustee began auctioning off the *aliyahs* to the Torah. Hasidim outbid one another. The trustee chanted, "Six gulden going once, six gulden going twice, six gulden . . . going . . . going . . . six gulden and ten . . ." As soon as the trustee had called out the last words, the convert screamed at the top of his lungs, "What's going on here? Money, money, money!"

He stamped his bare feet, waved his fists, and shouted, "Gulden, gulden, gulden . . . It's Yom Kippur! You boors! . . . You're sinning! It's a desecration of God's name!"

"Peasant!" someone screeched.

"A goy remains a goy," a youngster called out.

"You're a goy yourself," the convert replied. "Yom Kippur is a holy day. The holiest day of the year. God forgives our sins and you're doing business, business . . . just like they did in the Holy

Temple long ago . . . That's why it was destroyed . . . That's why the Messiah isn't coming!"

And the convert broke into tears—a hoarse, manly weeping that sent a shudder through everyone. The congregants fell silent.

Then the trustee called out, "We must support our *shtibl* . . . We need coal for the winter. We have to pay rent."

"On Yom Kippur one is forbidden to do business in the presence of the Torah," the convert replied.

"You don't have to teach us how to be Jews."

"It's forbidden," he said.

After a while the Hasidic *shtibl* got rid of the convert and he went to pray in a study house. But he still caused problems on the street. He preached morality to the prostitutes who stood by the gates. He went to the square where the thieves hung out and delivered a sermon half in Yiddish, half in Russian, showing them where in the Bible the phrase "Do not steal" appeared in the Ten Commandments. Even at that time there were homes on the street where women cooked on the Sabbath, and the convert went there to rebuke them, predicting catastrophes, epidemics, even pogroms. It wasn't long before the children were tagging after him and teasing him with "Ivan, Ivan, there you go. Ivan, Ivan, stub your toe!"

But his greatest outrage was reserved for the young girls who wore short-sleeved, low-cut dresses. The convert ran after them, called them wantons and whores; they were sinning, he shouted, and causing others to sin.

On the street there was a teahouse where boys and girls would gather on the Sabbath to crack pumpkin seeds, flirt, and dance. The proprietor went about with her hair uncovered and would occasionally pour cold water into the urn or surreptitiously push the iron poker into the fire. The convert, seeing what was going on, appointed himself guardian of Sabbath observance. The thieves and hooligans who frequented the place cursed the convert and told him he'd wake up one day with a knife in his back. The girls laughed at him and escorted him out of the teahouse with catcalls.

The convert complained to Father, rebuking him for not tending to the street. Father justified himself before the convert as if he were one of his own, telling him how little attention today's generation paid to ethical pronouncements. Father hinted to the convert that he should rather pray, learn to be a Jew, and not try to improve others, for it was wasted effort. But the convert pointed out to Father the verse in the Pentateuch where one is commanded to rebuke one's fellow man.

Father agreed, but showed him a law stating that if one knew for certain that one's moralizing would not be efficacious, and that the next fellow was sinning wantonly and willfully, then one should no longer preach to him. "Everything has its limit," Father declared.

"Because of them the Messiah won't come and we'll remain in exile forever."

"Forever? God forbid!"

"They're inviting a new destruction."

The convert refused to be consoled. The sinning on the street caused him endless anguish. His pale eyes shone with a non-Jewish bitterness.

One Sabbath people witnessed another bizarre scene: the convert was being led away, flanked by two police officers. Because it was forbidden in Russia to convert to Judaism, the convert had committed a crime against the regime. Apparently someone had informed on him to the authorities. Or perhaps he had committed another offense. The police closed his workshop, hung a lock on the door, and sealed it.

Some Jews suggested that they should make inquiries and find a lawyer for the convert, but no one had any money or time for such endeavors. After a while the lock on his door was removed and a soda-water shop opened up. The convert seemed to have vanished. Only now did the people on the street begin to understand what had happened. A goy had sacrificed his life for Yiddishkeit and Jews had mocked him. He was locked up somewhere and no one was making any effort to free him. Some said that the convert had been sent to Siberia. The cheder lads concluded that he had been either hanged or burned at the stake and that his soul had expired with the words "Hear O Israel." People on the street felt guilty.

They thought that they would never see the convert again. But not long after the Germans occupied Warsaw during World War I, a youth named Chaim told the following story:

Walking along Dluga Street one day he felt hungry. He saw a shop with Hebrew lettering. A young man stood in the doorway and asked Chaim, "You're hungry, eh? Then come in."

Chaim entered. He was served a bowl of grits and a heel of a bread. Other young men sat at a long table. After the meal a bareheaded Jew with the beard of a teacher and the gold-rimmed glasses of a rich man entered and began preaching: The true Messiah had already come and his name was Jesus of Nazareth. This Jew then talked about the little lamb, the paschal sacrifice, and Isaiah's prophecy that a virgin would become pregnant and give birth to a son. He explained the difficult verse in Psalms 2:12 by saying that it meant: kiss God's son.

Chaim then realized that he had fallen into a den of missionaries but he was afraid to abandon his meal and flee. Suddenly the convert appeared. It seemed that he lived there among them.

Yes, Jews had driven him away and he had gone over to the missionaries. "I'm a Jew. A Jew!" the convert asserted. "But the Messiah is already here. You're waiting in vain. Jesus is the Messiah . . . Jesus of Nazareth!"

When this story was repeated back in the *shtibl*, the Jews there declared, "That's the problem with goyim. They don't have the patience to wait."

A CHUNK OF DARKNESS

ഗ്രെ

The door opened and an old woman with a cane entered. She was not white but black: she had a black, disheveled marriage wig; a dark, wrinkled face; black eyes; a little black beard on the tip of a prominent double chin—and she wore a black shawl and a black dress so long it seemed to sweep the floor after her. Old age is usually associated with repose and quietude, but the old age of this woman was as dark as a witch's. She was full of beardlike tufts of hair and warts.

But, in fact, she spoke about Jewish matters. She was old, she said. She had saved a little money, which she would not use up during her lifetime. Since she was childless, she wanted to hire a fine man who in a hundred years would say Kaddish in her memory. She proposed that my father should do this and she was prepared to advance him one hundred rubles. The rest would be paid after her funeral.

We needed the money, but my father declined. He said that nobody knows whose tomorrow it will be. How could he take money from her? No one has a contract with the Master of the

Universe. I sensed that Father had other reservations. He did not want to derive income from somebody else's death, even if it was an old woman's. The whole matter was distasteful to him.

But the old woman did not relent. Who could help her if not the rabbi, she exclaimed, banging her cane on the floor. Father considered who should assume this responsibility and quickly found the right person. In the Hasidic *shtibl* there was a small man with a little gray beard, a florid face, and young eyes. Although he was no longer young, he still had a lively gait. He often drank, spun stories, and joked around. It was clear that he was healthy, thank God, and had many years left to live. He had been a small-time merchant, but now his son-in-law, a wealthy fruit wholesaler, supported him. Father sent for this man. When Father informed him of the old woman's request, the man immediately agreed. Rubbing his reddish hands, he said, "Why not? Kaddish is Kaddish."

The old woman glared at him darkly. Her black eyes seemed to drill into him, probing his innermost secrets. After a moment she called out, "I also want him to lead the prayer service in my memory."

"Why not? I'll lead the service."

"An entire year!" the old woman blurted out angrily.

"Certainly, all year long."

"And on the anniversary of my death I want a memorial candle lit and I want you to study Mishnah."

"I study Mishnah anyway . . ."

"I want a contract and a handshake."

Here Father finally intervened: "We can have a signed agreement, but a handshake is not necessary. When a Jew makes a promise he keeps his word, God willing."

"You, Rabbi, would keep your promise, but I don't trust him!" the woman said with a vigor that belied her age.

"If you don't trust him, then it's no good," Father said. "In such a matter one must trust the other person to keep his word."

"Rabbi, you I'll trust."

The gray man stood all the while with an expression that said, Whichever way it goes, I can manage without her . . . He wore a cotton-lined gray gaberdine, a little plush hat, a red scarf around his neck, and a pair of leather boots that looked indestructible. His red cheeks, lined with little veins, bore witness that he enjoyed his drink and was full of life's juices. He took out a little snuffbox, poured a bit of snuff onto the palm of his hand, and then drew it deeply into his hairy nostrils. He did not even sneeze. We cheder boys used to say that not sneezing is a sure sign the snuff has gone straight to your brain . . .

Eventually they drew up a contract and the man signed it. When he suggested that they seal the deal with a glass of brandy, the old woman sent me down to buy a bottle and some egg biscuits. The man poured himself a large drink and the woman took a glass herself. Father did not drink. The man, the Kaddish sayer, raised another large glass and called out, "Now that you have somebody to say Kaddish after you, may you live to be one hundred and twenty!"

The old woman shook her head. "What's the good of my life?"

She had been prepared to give my father one hundred rubles in advance, but gave only twenty-five to the old man, promising the balance after her death. The old man acquiesced to everything and then left.

The woman stayed; she went into the kitchen and insinuated to my mother that she wasn't satisfied with this deal. She had no trust in this person. My mother heard her out and said, "The best thing is to say Kaddish for oneself."

"How, my dear, can one say Kaddish for oneself?"

"One does deeds of charity. One prays. One observes Yiddishkeit. One does not speak ill of other people. All of this is better than the best Kaddish."

The old woman pondered this, then left.

A couple of months passed. Suddenly the door opened and the old woman limped in, black as a crow. Even her nose resembled a crow's beak.

"Rebbetzin, I've been hoodwinked."

"What happened?"

"The shmendrick's getting married, of all things!"

Apparently the old man, her Kaddish sayer, was preparing to marry a hunk of tripe who sold rotten apples in the marketplace.

At first Mother was surprised; then she asked, "What's the harm in that? Since he promised to say Kaddish, he'll say it."

"His wife won't let him."

"Why wouldn't she let him?"

"Because she's a bitch."

The woman stubbornly insisted that we send for her Kaddish sayer. I didn't have to run too far, for all of this took place in our courtyard. The man was sitting in the *shtibl* telling stories. He came right away. As soon as he saw the old woman, his eyes twinkled.

"What does she want now?"

The old woman maintained that since he was getting married she regretted the entire deal.

"Regret is not businesslike," the old man responded.

The old woman wanted her twenty-five rubles back, but the man said he had already spent them. He impatiently shuffled his thick-soled leather boots, then yelled, "What a shlimazel!"

It was not an easy lawsuit. The man denied nothing. He had already eaten up the money. He had made no agreement with this old woman that he was not allowed to marry. There was no room for compromise here because the man was unwilling to return even a broken kopeck. Father said that the man's marriage was no obstacle to his saying Kaddish. How is one thing connected to the other? But the old woman was angry. Her muttering and mumbling portended no good. She glowered darkly at the man. It seemed to me she wanted to give him the evil eye and was casting a spell over him to destroy him.

"I'll have to hire another man," she called out.

"Why another? I'll say Kaddish for you."

"I don't want your Kaddish."

"Then no is no."

"That money of mine will make him miserable," the old woman predicted gloomily.

The old man got married. A couple of weeks after the wedding he came to the *shtibl.* His red cheeks had yellowed. He was hunched over. His boots now seemed much too big for him.

The men in the *shtibl* joked with him: "Well, how's our young man doing?"

The man spit on the ground. "No good."

"What's up?"

"A witch, everything rotten you can imagine."

"What does she want?"

"Who knows? She torments me. She doesn't let me sleep at night with her yapping. She wakes up the neighbors. People come knocking on the door."

"So what does she want?"

"I'll be darned if I know. She talks like a madwoman, may it not happen to us!"

"So what will you do? Go back to your daughter?"

"My daughter won't let me in."

"What's the matter?"

"She's angry that I married."

"So what will happen?"

"It's not a good situation."

The man had quarreled with his daughter and son-in-law, and married a half-crazy market woman. His little gray beard had turned entirely white.

He stopped telling stories. He sat in the *shtibl* and mournfully chanted psalms, as if for a dangerously ill person. On several occasions he did not return home to sleep. The shamesh would find him in the morning stretched out on a bench with a no-longer-usable tallis under his head.

After a while people heard that he had divorced the market woman but that his daughter still refused to let him enter her house. He had exchanged her mother for a vulgar market harridan—and for this his daughter could not forgive him. The old man began making efforts to be admitted to the old-age home but there was told he was too young. Moreover, one also had to bring a dowry like—forgive the comparison—a nun who wants to enter a cloister.

Then the old woman with the little black beard reappeared. She began to cook grits for him, darn his socks, and launder his shirts and his long johns. She became his protector. This woman, for whom he was supposed to say Kaddish, had started to act like his wife.

It didn't take long for the inevitable to occur. The old woman came to us and announced that she was prepared to marry this man who should have said Kaddish for her and was surely twenty years her junior.

As she spoke she pounded the floor with her cane. Her little beard shook. The warts on her face bobbed quickly. It isn't hard for a woman to be alone, she maintained. Why does she need a man? She cooks some food in a little pot, does a bit of laundry, sweeps her apartment, and everything is the way it ought to be. When she gets an occasional bellyache at night, she heats up a pot lid and places it on her stomach. But a man is like an abandoned child. He can't cook, he can't do laundry, he can't clean up. If one doesn't tend to him, he neglects himself completely. Since he would say Kaddish for her anyway, he might as well become her husband. She had an apartment and a bit of money. Surely he wouldn't starve. "The couple of years I have left to me, let's live them out decently," she added.

Mother listened to her and was silent. The old man came also. He wasn't overly anxious for this match, but he said, "Do I have a choice? My daughter doesn't want me, so somebody has to take pity on me . . . and I no longer have the strength to sleep on a hard bench."

He married—but apparently did not strike gold. Once again he sat in the *shtibl* and mournfully chanted psalms.

The youngsters began questioning him. They wanted to know if he had dallied with the witch, but the old man snapped, "I'm not obliged to give you any reports!"

"How old is she?"

"I didn't count her years."

"Does she have a bundle?"

"Rascals! Back to your books!" the old man shouted.

One winter evening, between the Afternoon and Evening Services, the old man complained that he had a bad cold. He went home but did not return for prayers the next morning. The following morning he didn't come to the *shtibl* either. The Jews there began saying that they ought to pay him a sick call. But it was already too late—the Kaddish sayer had died.

At the funeral a quarrel broke out between the widow and the old man's daughter. After the shiva period, the old woman came to Father requesting that a new Kaddish sayer be found for her. Another thing: since her husband had left no son and since his son-in-law was a roughneck, a boor, a scoundrel, she was prepared to pay a few extra rubles for someone to say Kaddish for him.

The old woman stood in the kitchen, black as coal, with a distorted face, a drooping mouth—a chunk of darkness. She exuded a demonic power. My mother usually welcomed people amicably, but she displayed a repugnance toward this old murderer. Father said that he knew of no other Kaddish sayers and hinted that she leave him alone. But she did not leave right away. Her gaze radiated a fierce stubbornness, the eerie self-confidence of those who have lived too long and no longer have any fear of the Angel of Death. I was still a little boy at the time, but I clearly sensed that the old woman had in some secretive manner done in her Kaddish sayer. Like a spider she had enmeshed him in her web and destroyed him.

A RABBI NOT LIKE
MY FATHER

ॐ

From time to time a certain rabbi would come to visit my father. He looked nothing like Father: tall, broad, and stout, with a pitch-black beard and black, burning eyes, he was also better dressed. He wore a fur coat with tails during the winter—and a wide silken topcoat in summer. He always had a new hat and was never without a parasol. He also smoked cigars. He brought into our house the prestige of a successful rabbi for whom everything was going well.

But things were not going as well as they appeared. He had once been a rabbi in a rather large city, but for some reason he had been relieved of his rabbinic duties. Now he lived in Warsaw and was for all intents and purposes no more than a small-time rabbi like my father. But the rich man's bearing stayed with him nevertheless. He wore chamois half-boots with rubber soles. He smoked his cigars through an amber cigar holder. His parasol had a silver handle. And his hands were thickly grown with hair, which by itself was a sign of wealth.

How different he was from my father! He came in softly, slowly removed his galoshes (which had brass monograms), put his umbrella in a corner, and the kitchen was soon filled with the smell of his cigar. He cast a sidelong glance at my mother. In the study he sat down warily, as if the chair were not sturdy enough. Father welcomed him warmly, as he did everyone, and asked Mother to bring in tea and biscuits. The rabbi took off his hat, under which sat a high yarmulke.

"How are you doing?" Father asked.

Those were about the only words that Father managed to utter during the entire visit. The rabbi began talking and continued for several hours. He spoke only of himself and his greatness. He neither praised himself openly nor spoke ill of others, but all his remarks had only one meaning: that he, the rabbi, was the greatest scholar of their generation and that all the other rabbis were either total or half ignoramuses who didn't understand what they were studying and merely skimmed the surface of issues. The rabbi spoke only about his books, his new interpretations, his accomplishments. His sharp eyes emitted the contempt and mockery of someone who knows everything better than everyone else but feels that the world begrudges him his success and refuses to acknowledge it out of envy.

I stood behind Father's chair and listened. Sometimes Father tried to say something, but the rabbi wouldn't let him speak. He made a hand motion that seemed to say: What do you know? What could you possibly have to say about such matters? It's enough of an honor for you that I come here and speak to you.

The rabbi did other things that surely must have irked Father. When referring to a certain passage in the Talmud, he would translate every single word, as though my father were just a little cheder lad. My father had by then written several scholarly commentaries and had already been a rabbi in a city. There was surely no need to translate anything for him. Often, this conceited rabbi translated passages from the Talmud for my father which even I, a little boy, understood. I blushed with embarrassment. I thought that Father would stand up and tell him to go to the devil, but I saw no sign on my father's face that he took offense. He listened to that man's exegesis with curiosity, as though he, my father, were a simple man for whom everything had to be spelled out. It actually seemed that Father took particular delight from the way the other man was translating everything into Yiddish.

Once, after the rabbi cited a Talmudic passage and immediately began to explain it, Father interrupted: "I'm afraid you've made a mistake."

The rabbi turned red, then paled. "I made a mistake?"

Father quickly began justifying himself. "Well, we ought to look at the text. Sometimes one can make a mistake." And Father quoted the Biblical verse: "Who can understand errors? . . . Everyone can make a mistake."

I thought that the rabbi would go to the bookcase, take out a Talmud folio, and look up the passage—but he did not do this and changed the topic instead. Evidently it wasn't appropriate for him to admit that my father could have caught him erring. He continued to sit there, speaking about himself while smoking his cigar. Every once in a while Mother brought in more tea and lemon.

It was very awkward when women entered the study to ask a question about *kashrus* during his visit. The housewife had come in to see Father, of course, but it was the other rabbi, the guest, who immediately took up the question. He turned to the woman, asking how big the soup pot was and how much milk had fallen into it. In another instance, when there was some doubt about a chicken, he waited for Father to cut open the navel where the woman had found a nail, or to inspect the guts, which were pockmarked. When Father had completed this "unsavory task," the rabbi took over and rendered his decision. I saw this as an act of great impudence, and it annoyed me, the little boy, terribly. I hoped that Father would say, I am the rabbi on this street, not you. But once again Father revealed not the slightest sign that he was annoyed. On the contrary, he amicably nodded his head to everything the rabbi said. When the woman left and bade them goodbye, only Father answered. Evidently it was beneath the rabbi's dignity to respond to an ordinary housewife.

Later, I looked up the mistake my father had caught. I showed Father that it was he who was right, not the rabbi. Father said, "Even the greatest people can make mistakes."

"Father, is he really such a genius?" I asked.

"He's a great scholar."

"Aren't there greater scholars?"

"Can Torah scholarship be measured? Everyone understands the Torah according to his ability. Sometimes one encounters a problem which a great scholar cannot answer while a simple Jew can. Everyone has a share in the Torah."

One time the rabbi came and seemed to be terribly angry. He had written a letter of approbation for a scholarly treatise and the author had not given him, the rabbi, the title that he thought he deserved. The author had called him "the *gaon*," that is, the genius, but had omitted the word "famous." On another letter of approbation the term "famous" had indeed been included. The rabbi maintained that all this concerned him as much as last year's snow. That little nothing of a scholar couldn't make him famous or not famous, the rabbi told Father. But it was the impudence, he said, that infuriated him. The rabbi made muck and mire of that scholar. He called him a boor, a thickhead, an ass, a donkey, a fool, a moron, an ox, and other similar names. He continued complaining: "He is as fit to be an author as I am to be a woodchopper. He should be an aleph-beys teacher, not a scholar. He's a simpleton, a common lout, a zero. Of people like him it is said: That which is wisdom isn't his writing and that which is his writing isn't wisdom. In short, he has taken everything from others. There isn't a thing in his book that's his own original work. The trouble is that he can't even properly steal from others. For that, one has to have a head on one's shoulders, but he has a clump of cabbage, not a head. And even that head of cabbage is all stem . . ."

Father was silent. His face was red. I later looked up that letter of approbation which this same rabbi had given to that scholar. He had written: "In his work the author uproots mountains. He is a library full of books. He has descended into the very depths of the Talmud and has come up with a pearl." This flowery language did not at all jibe with his abusive language. He was enraged that the author had not called him "famous."

That day the rabbi spoke longer than usual. Even I could see that this rabbi was capable of murder for that shortened honorific he had been given. Everything in him stormed and seethed. He smoked one cigar after another and the apartment filled with noxious wisps of smoke. He vented his rage at Father. Now not only did he explain each Talmud passage he mentioned but he even began explaining Biblical verses. Father sat there shrunken. It was absolutely impossible to respond, because the rabbi spewed such a thick barrage of words one couldn't even insert a "but." After the rabbi left, Father at once went to the Hasidic *shtibl*. It seemed to me he wanted to clear his head in the street a bit.

Another time the rabbi came to visit us after Father had published his own book, one with a letter of approbation from that same rabbi. When Father showed him the book, the rabbi glanced quickly at the honorific title that Father had given him, then at once began speaking about his own affairs. He did not congratulate Father, nor did he even attempt to cut open the pages and look into the book, which was customary on such occasions. His eyes brimmed with scorn and contempt. It seemed that the rabbi took the fact of Father's publishing a book as an insult. And another thing: in the period between the rabbi's visits, Father had spent some time in Bilgoray with his father-in-law, my grandfather. The rabbi knew quite well that Father had undertaken a journey, but he didn't even ask about it. For him, Father was merely a pair of ears. It sufficed him that Father should hear what he, the world-famous genius, had to say . . .

Mother declared that she wouldn't let the rabbi cross our threshold anymore, but Father implored her not to do such a thing, God forbid.

"He has his flaws, but he's a great scholar," Father said.

Then my mother uttered something I had never heard her say before: "Yes, he's great. He grates on one's nerves."

In time, the rabbi stopped visiting us. I grew up somewhat. Once, a scholar praised my father's book, telling me that Father "interprets what he sees." For him, the plain meaning of the text was more important than overly subtle hair-splitting. He compared Father to the early commentators. I then asked the scholar if he knew that rabbi who would come to visit us, and if he indeed was such a genius.

The scholar replied, "Disjointed blather . . . lots of hot air . . . In his quibbling analyses he tries to bring East and West together. Can you bring two walls together? Futile attempts . . . he doesn't even come up to your father's ankles."

SOUNDS THAT INTERFERE
WITH STUDYING

ဖ၈

A few doors from us there was an apartment whose tenants were dissolute. It wasn't a house of prostitution, God forbid, but the people who lived there were decidedly low-class. The man probably dealt in stolen goods; in Warsaw lingo he was called a fence. He may have had another profession which wasn't too kosher either. His wife went about bareheaded. In my parents' view, everything about that apartment was loud and brazen. The walls were colored rose and red. They had a gramophone that squeaked out all kinds of theater songs from early in the morning until late at night. They had a cage with canaries and a parrot. And as if that wasn't enough, they also kept a dog.

The man's wife was chubby, with big breasts, a short neck, and a round face. She didn't speak; she sang. Her Yiddish was a kind of Warsaw slang; she added letters to words and changed prefixes. She also spoke Polish. She had a baby girl whom she took out on walks in a stroller. We considered all these things gentile ways.

In that apartment they were still asleep at 10 a.m., for they went to bed at three in the morning. Aside from breakfast, lunch, and supper, they also took a second supper at midnight. Their gentile maid would go down late at night to bring them crackly fresh rolls, salami, turkey breast, liver, roast meat, goose, or a platter of cold cuts, all of which they dipped into mustard and washed down with beer. Sometimes they would eat hot sausages. And during this meal the men—the owner of the apartment and his guests—spoke loudly and shouted. The women's laughter could be heard in the entire courtyard.

Every manner of evil was imputed to them. The man shaved his beard. He didn't even attend synagogue on Sabbath. The woman did not go to the ritual bath. They had a balcony next to ours and on it they did all kinds of forbidden things. Men kissed women. They used uncouth expressions. My mother once saw the mistress of the house kissing her dog. "How low can people sink?" Mother asked. "That's what happens when people turn away from the Jewish path."

Once, they threw a party and invited the police. Father immediately removed his rabbinic hat and put on a velvet one with a high crown, for he did not have a permit to be a rabbi. He was afraid that while they were celebrating, the police might decide to inspect his apartment. The thought that Jews were sitting at one table with peasants, eating and drinking and having a good time, struck him as wild. How could one enjoy one's food when a peasant was sitting opposite you? How could the grandchildren of Abraham, Isaac, and Jacob be fraternizing with the enemies of Israel?

Father said, "Alas, it's all because of this dark and bitter exile that we're in. It's high time for the Messiah to come. It's time, high time!"

Mother also walked about the house upset. We heard men shouting, women laughing, and after a while the gramophone played a march and we could hear them dancing. Men and women were dancing together, and all of this was happening no more than a door or two away.

One day I saw some policemen going up to that apartment. I thought that our neighbors were having another party, but it was something entirely different. The owner of the apartment had been arrested. I saw him coming down, a tall man with a long face and a long neck, wearing a shirt without a collar. Strangely, a pair of brand-new boots bound by a string was hanging from his shoulders. The new boots fascinated me more than the fact of his arrest. One boot dangled over his chest, the other over his back. Was he going to stay in jail for years? Did he know in advance that he would be imprisoned? And if so, why didn't he run away?

His wife followed him, as did many others. Once outside, the policemen and our neighbor boarded a droshky and off they went—to prison, no doubt.

For a couple of days the apartment was quiet. Not a sound came from the gramophone, the dog, the parrot, or the canaries. A weird silence emanated from the rooms from which the owner had been taken. Father insinuated that perhaps now those people would repent, for if they were already being punished in this world, what had they gained? But he was mistaken.

Soon the gramophone was heard once again playing the same merry little tunes and ditties as before. Once again we heard the dog and the birds. And if that was not enough, a rumor circulated in the courtyard that the woman had taken a lover. A man began visiting. He wasn't as tall as the apartment owner, but he was broad-shouldered. He had a wide nose, a thick mustache, and the eyes of a libertine. He wore a Polish jacket and a pair of baggy riding breeches. His boots had such narrow uppers it was hard to imagine how a man's foot could slip into them. He always came with presents in hand: all kinds of small packages tied with colored ribbons and held with little wooden handles.

Mother came into Father's study and said, "These things are unheard of even among respectable gentiles . . . an adulterous woman!"

"I don't want to hear about it! Enough!" Father replied.

"It's like getting slapped in the face when I look at them!"

"So don't look! What's there to look at?"

"Perhaps you should summon her to your courtroom."

Father sighed. First of all, he knew that anything he said would do no good; second, he didn't want to hear the voice of such a wanton. He said, "She would defile the apartment."

"One must warn someone before imposing punishment!" Mother answered, quoting the Talmud.

Father placed his handkerchief on the Talmud he was studying. "Who should summon her?"

"Mama, I'll go."

Father cast an angry glance at me. "I don't want you to have anything to do with such people."

But there was no one else to go. Furthermore, if a stranger went, the woman would surely pay him no heed. I heard Mother telling Father, "What does he know? He doesn't know a thing . . ."

"Well then, all right."

They told me to summon the woman, and I went off at once. I was a bit afraid of the dog, but my curiosity to see this dissolute apartment was greater than my fear. As soon as I knocked on the door, I heard the dog barking. Then I saw the mistress of the house. She wore an unbuttoned, lace-decorated housecoat and a pair of wide bloomers also adorned with lace. I could see her breasts, too. She stood next to me, a hunk of evil impulse, Rehab the prostitute, a Biblical harlot, a half-naked piece of riffraff. All kinds of unkosher smells emanated from her. The entire woman was one chunk of *trayf*ness. My nose was subjected to such awful smells I couldn't even speak.

"Papa is summoning you!" I barely managed to say.

"And who's your papa?"

"The rabbi."

"What does the rabbi need me for?"

And she began to laugh, displaying a set of broad teeth. Here and there a piece of gold glinted. Her lover came into the room; he wore no jacket but had on a gold, polka-dotted little vest. The parrot began screeching. The dog began barking again.

The man asked, "What does the little jerk want?"

"I'm being summoned to the rabbi."

"Tell his father to go fly a kite," the man responded, slamming the door in my face.

I left, stung to the core. I told my parents what I had seen. Father said in Aramaic, "Since he has so much impudence, it's obvious that he's a bastard." In this fashion Father took his revenge upon the wanton by quoting a line from the Gemara.

Nevertheless, half an hour later the neighbor came to our apartment. Father began lecturing her, but the woman denied everything.

"Never mind what people say," she said. "People have big yaps, so they shoot off their mouths. Let 'em babble, let 'em blab with their behinds. Let 'em spit up blood and pus. Sure, as if I've got nothing better to think about when my husband is sitting in the clinker than another man! . . . May their bones rot! A fire in their kishkes!"

"One is forbidden to curse."

"Rabbi, it's the truth."

"One is forbidden to curse even if it's the truth."

"Rabbi, I'm a kosher wife. It's all a lie. There's not one bit of truth in it. He's my husband's good friend, so he comes into the house to hear news. What should I do? Throw him out?"

"God forbid."

"Then what?"

"It is written that one is forbidden to give people the opportunity to be suspicious."

"Is it my fault that people have big eyes? May their eyes go blind, dear sweet Father in heaven!"

Father apparently believed her, because he went on: "Why do you keep a dog? It's not a Jewish trait."

"Rabbi, the street is full of thieves. If not for the dog, I'd be in the poorhouse."

You're full of baloney! You're talking through your hat, I thought to myself. You can pick a pocket just by looking. But Father became milder and milder. He said, "One doesn't live forever. It is written that when a person dies, God forbid, neither

49

silver nor gold accompanies him. Not precious stones and pearls but only *mitzvahs* and good deeds."

"Don't you think I know this? I have a little charity box hanging in my kitchen. I light candles every Friday night. Every day I put in a couple of coins. May my husband come back to me in good health! . . ."

Before she left Father wished her well.

As soon as she had departed, Mother came in. "Well, what have you accomplished?"

"She denies everything."

"And do you believe her?"

"People dream up all kinds of stories."

Mother was annoyed with Father, saying that anyone could fool him. Then she quoted a Biblical verse to him that was hardly complimentary. He sat there with his head bent. By nature he trusted people and didn't like to delve into sins and wickedness. He had but one wish: to return to studying his sacred text.

A couple of months later the woman's husband was released from jail, but her lover—that's what they still called him on the street—kept coming to the apartment. The gramophone played on, the dog barked, the parrot screeched, and the canaries trilled. Again they gave a party and, evidently, once more invited the police. It was summertime and hot in our apartment, but Father ordered me to close the windows and said, "Why are you wandering about? Go study a Gemara."

QUESTION OR ADVICE?

ႸᏯ

The door opened and a young man entered. He was bent over like an old man, beardless, wearing a black suit with tin buttons and a hat with a leather brim. His eyes shone with suffering and stubbornness. His face was bronze-colored and his cheeks hollow. His entrance frightened my mother a bit, for his footfalls were not heard on the steps. He just stood there and did not say a word.

"What do you want?"

"Is the rabbi here?"

"He's in the study."

"What's the good word?" Father asked unceremoniously.

"Rabbi, my wife is a whore," the newcomer called out.

Only now did Father raise his eyes from the Gemara he was studying. Confused, he placed a narrow black cord on the page, then took out his handkerchief and wiped his brow.

"What are you talking about?"

"Rabbi, I'm not making it up. She's got a lover who spends days and nights in our house. She kisses him right in front of me. When I leave, he creeps into her bed . . ."

51

"*Nu, nu, nu* . . . tsk tsk tsk," Father muttered. He looked around, apparently suspicious that I was in the room. But I was standing behind the bookcase, which was perpendicular to the wall, and he couldn't see me. And besides, he was nearsighted. For a while he sat staring into his text as though ashamed. Then he said, "Why do you let such a person into your apartment?"

"She takes in anybody she wants. She wears the pants in the family, not me."

"What do you do?"

"I'm a gravedigger. Not in the cemetery on Genshe Street* but in the one in Praga. That's where I work."

Father wiped the perspiration from his forehead. "*Nu* . . ."

"I'm not home all day long. Sometimes I go out early in the morning and don't come back till very late at night. Sometimes there are a lot of dead people. So she does what she wants. She lives with him openly and makes a laughingstock of me!"

"Stick her with a divorce!" Father shouted. "You are not allowed to remain under one roof with such a promiscuous woman!"

"Rabbi, she denies it completely."

"What do you mean, she denies it? You yourself just said you've seen it with your own eyes."

"I saw them kissing, but not—like they say—not the real thing."

---

*Between the world wars Warsaw had two Jewish cemeteries: the older one in Praga (on the other side of the Vistula River) for the poor and the other at the end of Genshe Street, where the richer people were buried. (Author)

"That is enough. A married woman who kisses another man is a whore!" Father raised his voice again. "She deserves to be divorced without a settlement."

"She doesn't want to divorce me."

"Put the bill of divorce in her hands. You are not allowed to be with her one minute longer."

"Even if she only kisses him?"

"Yes. One thing leads to another. Even if a woman is just running around, one may divorce her. The Gemara calls someone like that a prostitute. A Jewish girl doesn't run around and doesn't consort with strange men. Woe unto us, it's awful!"

"Rabbi, we have two children. Two decent girls."

"Take the children away from her. With such a mother the children will grow up to be licentious, God forbid. Why didn't you speak up before?" Father was roused again.

"I always thought she would come to her senses. After all, it's not easy to destroy one's home."

"In such matters there's no such thing as 'coming to one's senses,'" Father said. "Of course, one can repent any deed, but when a married woman has dealings with a strange man, she becomes defiled. Who is he, this sinner of Israel? Why did you let him into your home in the first place?"

"Rabbi, he's a human being, not a wild beast. We met, we struck up a friendship, my wife invited him over. He comes, he talks, we drink a glass of brandy together. We play cards. He owns flat wagons and has people working for him. Mine is a strange line of work, Rabbi. There's income, but we just barely manage. The men who do the burying receive a big salary. I dig out the grave and they get the money. Among normal folk a man comes home, tells his wife what he did during the day and how it went. What can I tell her? As soon as I come into the house she shouts, 'Wash your hands!' But my hands are clean! My children are ashamed of how I make a living. What should I do? After all, it's a sure way of making a gulden. *Nu*, so we sit down together and have a bit of fun."

"What do you mean 'together'?"

"Me, she, and him."

"Well, so then you yourself are responsible."

"One can't always be alone."

"Don't you have any family?"

"I have family, but I can't talk to them."

"Why not? Do you go to *shul*?"

"Sometimes, on a Sabbath."

"A Jew has to pray three times a day! When you go to a *shul* or a study room, you're already among people. A woman has neighbors. How do all Jews live? The Gemara says that when a person goes into a tannery, a stench envelops him. And since you are taking a libertine into your house and you and your wife play cards with him, it can only lead to sinning."

"Rabbi, I'm not a fanatic."

"I don't know what you're talking about."

"Like people say, we don't live today the way they lived one hundred years ago."

"The Master of the Universe is the same as He was one hundred and one thousand years ago, and the Torah is also the same. That is how goyim behave, not Jews. A Jewish daughter must be modest."

"So what should I do, Rabbi?"

"So you have actually seen her—how did you put it?—kissing him?"

"Yes, Rabbi. Not once, but a hundred times."

"And since she behaves with such chutzpah right in front of you, what do you think she does later?"

"Rabbi, it's an open secret."

"Divorce her! Divorce her! You're not allowed to stay with her even a minute longer. She's also forbidden to marry that other one. That's the law!"

"Rabbi, he has a wife."

"Really? ... *Nu* ..."

"She won't give me the children."

"First of all, you yourself must get rid of her. Every minute you continue to live with her is a sin. Let her think it over and repent. Such things don't happen to Jews who follow the right path. It all stems from modern behavior. A Jew must have a beard and sidecurls; he must go to *shul* and pray, study a chapter of Mishnah, or whatever he can. A Jewish wife must shave her head and follow the laws of family purity and other *mitzvahs*. The things you've described do not happen to upright Jews. They happen only to promiscuous people."

"Yes, Rabbi, my mother, may she rest in peace, never even looked at anyone else. For her there was only one God and one man."

"Well, so you see for yourself."

"But still, I can't be like my father."

"Why not? The Torah is not in heaven. Everybody can be a Jew."

"Yes, but ..."

Silence fell. Father covered his eyes with his hand and held it there for a while. His mild face became stern. A wrinkle appeared on his high forehead. Aside from hating sins and licentiousness, Father apparently couldn't understand how a man could permit his wife, the mother of his children, to dally with another man. Father continued, saying that this went against the natural order. Only sinners turn the natural order upside down. As the man listened to Father, he became even more stooped over. He looked as though he might break in two.

"What should I do, Rabbi?"

"Call her to a rabbinic judgment."

"She won't come."

"Let a divorce bill be written and hand it to her. Do you have a civil marriage license?"

"Marriage license? No."

"Divorce her and never again look at her defiled face!"

The gravedigger began to make faces and cough. He cast a questioning look at me, the little boy. Father was as decisive as this man was full of doubts. The man looked both vexed and overflowing with a kind of softness I couldn't grasp. It seemed that he had not revealed everything. There were some untold secrets and that's why we couldn't make head or tail of his story. He began speaking partly to Father and partly to himself.

"Such things can't be done quickly. After all, we've been living together sixteen years. We have two nice children. How are they to blame, the poor things? She's fallen in love, fallen in love. He's a braggart the like of which you can't find in Warsaw. He's a handsome young man with a smooth tongue. People say that a woman is long on hair and short on brains. She doesn't want to think about it. She chased him away once, but then she asked me to go and apologize to him."

"And you went to apologize to him?!"

"It's gloomy at home and when he comes he brings some joy into the house. He brings us a bottle of brandy, this, that, and the other thing. He has lots of stories to tell. Maybe none of them are true, but meanwhile, we laugh and joke around. He also sings well and my wife likes to sing, too."

"Enough! I don't want to hear any more! You're to blame for everything!" Father shouted. "If one plays with fire, one gets burned. You're a stubborn rebel! And you're not even repentant or prepared to change your behavior. So why did you come to me? I can only tell you what the law states!"

"Rabbi, I'm miserable."

"In the next world you'll be even more miserable, God forbid. A person does not live forever. She's an adulteress—and you're the cause of it! This is one of the three sins of which it is said: 'It is better to be killed than to sin: forbidden sex, idol worship, and murder.' For any other sin one is forbidden to give up one's life, because the Torah holds a person's life precious. And since the Torah has ordained that one should let oneself be killed for this type of conduct, you can readily understand how heinous is this sin."

"Yes, Rabbi, I know."

"So if you know, why do you remain silent?"

"It's just that I think things over. All of this. All along I thought perhaps she would change her mind. I spoke to her about it. What will people say? People are laughing into their fists. The children are growing up and they understand everything. My younger daughter is quite smart. She has a mature outlook. Every word of hers is a delight. She loves me. Him she can't stand. He brings her little chocolates, but she refuses them. She's my daughter and she takes after me. So I say to my wife, What's the upshot going to be? But she hasn't got the faintest idea. If he doesn't show up one day, she's totally out of sorts. The only thing she's afraid of is that he'll find himself another woman. The truth is, Rabbi, that he has ten others. That's the sort of nature he has. Seeing a skirt gets him all excited. I, Rabbi, I'm a settled sort of person. I, if I have a wife, I don't run after anybody else. So I say, What's going to be? It's like talking to the wall! All he has to do is say the word and she'd run off to America with him. She's been seduced by him, Rabbi. Completely seduced!"

"All the wicked are seduced! But you are forbidden to live with her."

"Perhaps we can still make peace. For the sake of the children."

Father made a motion as if to stand. "You're killing your children, too. When the children see that you know all this and remain silent, they assume that everything is fine."

"Does that mean it would be better for me to leave home and abandon everything?"

"Is that what you call a home? The Gemara says that a person may not live with a snake in one basket—"

"Yes, Rabbi, that's how it is: a snake . . . Good night, Rabbi."

"What? Oh, good night. A good year!"

"I'll think everything over."

"Well . . ."

When the man left, I came out from behind the bookcase.

"You were here all along?"

"I was looking for a book."

"And you heard everything?"

"I didn't pay attention."

"It's better that way. Better that way. Unfortunately, sinners are very stupid!"

And Father removed the narrow black cord from the Gemara and resumed studying.

BACK FROM ABROAD

ʂϾϿ

The door opened and a couple came in. The young man was tall with a short, trimmed beard. His neatness and modern garb had the look of someone who usually dressed more traditionally but was now on his way to America or to a spa. With his black fedora and parasol in hand he looked like a matchmaker or a cantor. Next to him stood a short woman. Her marriage wig, adorned with a broad hairband, was so small it looked like her own hair. She had a young girl's rosy cheeks and was rather chubby and round; it seemed she was all flesh and no bones. She clung to the tall man like a little girl.

"Do you perform marriages here?" he asked.

"Yes," Mother replied.

"How long does it take?"

"As quickly as you wish."

"Well, how much does it cost?"

"Five rubles."

"All right."

The young man smiled at the woman. Apparently he had expected it to cost more.

"Who are the bride and groom?" Mother asked.

"I am the groom and she is my bride," the young man replied. "Bride and groom are usually shy, but we have no reason to be. We were once married for six years already."

"You're not a Kohen*?" Mother asked.

"No, I'm an Israelite."

"And she has never remarried?"

The young man laughed. "Rebbetzin, do you think I'm an ignoramus? I know the law. I once studied in a yeshiva. The man who stands before you, even though he is wearing modern clothes, was close to getting rabbinic ordination. But I wanted to go abroad and she didn't want to leave her mama. So we divorced and I went to Antwerp, where I became a diamond cutter. But what good are diamonds to me if I left the true diamond in Poland? I couldn't sleep at night. I tossed and turned like someone with a high fever. Then I did a foolish thing while there and got married . . ."

The short woman grimaced coquettishly and said, "Why do you have to tell them all this?"

"So what! She didn't bite off a piece of me. It didn't work out and that's that. Her father was a slaughterer and made a good living over there. He wanted to make me a *shochet* as well. But how could I slaughter other creatures when I had already slaughtered myself. I missed her so much I thought I'd go out of my mind. I would occasionally hear about love and I just

---

*A Kohen, a member of the priestly class, from the tribe of Levi, is not permitted to marry a divorcée or a widow.

considered it the kind of nonsense written up in the papers. But I'm in love with this little woman standing next to me. I can't live without her, and that's the truth!"

"Oh, you're talking too much," the short woman said flirtatiously. "What difference does it make to them?"

"It makes a difference," Mother said. "There's a moral teaching that counsels that one must not rush into a divorce. What would you have done if, God forbid, she had gotten married, too? That would have been the end of it."

The short woman spoke up. "Me marry? I swore to myself that once is enough. People suggested matches to me. The matchmakers ran after me. My good mother even arranged a meeting with one of the men. But as soon as I took one look at him I thought, He's nothing like my husband, Berish, and I ran away!"

"Do you hear, Rebbetzin?"

"Well, it's good that a young couple is in love," Mother said. "That's how it should be. Still, one should not be in a hurry . . ."

But the young couple *was* in a hurry. Father wanted to postpone the wedding for a day, but the young man refused to consider it. He went out to buy sponge cake and brandy. I went down to look for a minyan. In the meantime, Father began filling out the printed marriage contract. As the woman sat on the chair her face changed colors. Someone loved her. Because of her someone had divorced his wife and cast aside a life of working with diamonds to return to her. She played with the stones of her amber necklace. On one finger a diamond sparkled.

Mother asked, "Is the diamond from here?"

"From there," the woman answered. "He brought it as a present."

"What do your parents say?"

"To tell you the truth, they don't want him," the woman began hesitantly. "Why did he run away so quickly? I love him, but I also love my mama and papa. I didn't want to put hundreds of miles between us. But once an idea gets into his head, it drives him crazy. So he ran and divorced me. What do you think? You think the *shochet*'s daughter accepted a divorce for nothing? He probably had to pay her off quite handsomely. Everything he saved up during the couple of years he was away went to the devil."

"Do you have any children?"

"We have an eight-year-old girl."

"And doesn't he have children with the other woman?"

"He says no. But who knows? He began writing letters, but I didn't answer them. My mama used to grab the letters and tear them up right away! She told the mailman to return all letters from Antwerp. But then he began sending the letters to his cousin, who brought them to me. I read them and saw at once that he had fallen into a pit. He missed me so much it was awful. And I longed for him, too. And the child kept asking, Where's Papa? Rebbetzin, I tell you, it was terrible. When Mama heard he was coming back, she made such a tumult you could hear it all over town. But I still don't have a hankering for anyone else. Papa is a mild-mannered man. He understood everything, but somehow it wasn't appropriate to get married again in our hometown. How would you put it? Father married Mother again? . . . They even sang a ditty about us in town."

"Things like that happen," Mother said.

"Yes, anything can happen. Rebbetzin, I forgot to ask you—
someone told me that he can use my ring. I don't have a new
wedding ring."

"If you give it to him as a gift, he'll be able to use it."

"How do I give it to him?"

"You declare that you're giving it to him as a gift."

"Well, that's fine with me."

The young man returned with surprising speed. He had
bought much more sponge cake and brandy than a minyan
could eat or drink. Meanwhile, I had scratched together part
of a minyan: a porter with a rope around his hips, an old man
who sat in the *shtibl* and recited psalms, a youth wearing torn
boots and disheveled sidecurls, a short man who sold hot
chickpeas and beans on the street, and an ordinary Jew with
a yellow beard whose sunburned face was full of freckles. But
these men did not suffice for the quorum of ten. So I went
off to round up some neighbors. The tailor, whose daughter
had died and whose son-in-law had married her sister, came
in white shirtsleeves, wearing glasses on the tip of his nose
and a measuring tape around his neck. Father told him to put
on a gaberdine and he returned wearing someone else's garment from which the basting threads had not yet been
removed.

I also called in the goose dealer from the third floor. While I
was gathering the minyan, the young groom had already told
every one of them his story. He looked half dizzy with joy. He
didn't stop talking, narrating, pointing to the short woman for
whom he had dragged himself from one train to another,
crossed borders, and brought ruination upon himself and others.

Then he remarked, "I'll be darned if I know what I'll do the morning after the wedding . . . I'm flat broke."

"You could have taken a young girl and gotten another dowry," the woman interjected.

"A dowry certainly wouldn't have poisoned me, but I don't need a young girl. In my eyes you are far better than the most beautiful girl. After all, I'm not the high priest who must marry a virgin. With God's help we'll scrape up a livelihood."

"That's exactly what I say."

"I always thought that a foreign country would be paradise," he said. "No small thing—being abroad! But once I crossed the border and saw that the sky is the same, the earth is the same, and the people are the same, I began to feel sad. That's how it is with everything. I thought that polishing diamonds would be clean work. No small thing—diamonds! But your hands get so filthy you can barely wash them clean. It's not much better than being a tanner. I'd be fine if at least there were steady work throughout the year. But no! It's seasonal. One day you're working and the next you're out of a job. There's a café in Antwerp where the jewel merchants meet. They gather at the little tables, and one man shows the next some sample diamonds wrapped in paper. The other man takes out his loupe, examines the gem, rubs it, and gives it to a third one. That one gives it to another. And so that little piece of paper goes from one hand to the next. These businessmen make a living, but the worker is afraid to buy a cup of coffee, for he may not have enough money for the tram ride home. Meanwhile, the *shochet*'s daughter sidled up to me. The *shochet* is a Polish Jew, one of our own, but over there he was already wearing a modern fedora. He wanted to make a *shochet* out of me. I had already started studying *Tevuos Shor*, but even as I sat with that book in my hands I was thinking about this woman . . ."

"*Nu*, that's quite enough!" Father said.

"What's the matter? Is it forbidden to love? Jacob also loved Rachel . . ."

"That story is an allegory!"

"The Talmud states: 'A verse in Scripture must be read in its literal sense.' Jacob simply loved her. When he woke up in the morning and saw Leah, he felt the disappointment down to his belly button."

"Come now, that's no way to talk!"

"Rabbi, I've taken a drop of brandy. I'm drunk—that's why I'm talking like that. Now that I've lived to see the day that I marry her, I feel it's Simchas Torah."

"Let's hear what you have to say a year from now, God willing," his wife said.

"I'll never divorce you again. I'd rather die a thousand deaths."

"Stop it, you're embarrassing me in front of all these people."

"What's the embarrassment? We're not strangers to each other."

During the ceremony, the woman cried. She covered her face with a kerchief. Father recited the blessings and gave the bride and groom a sip of wine from the goblet. Afterward, the young man seized his former wife and began kissing her. He even tried dancing with her. She tore away from him, but he said, "Now it's permitted."

He gave the men of the minyan large slices of sponge cake and poured out full glasses of brandy. He too drank. He grew more and more excited. The woman went into the kitchen to speak to Mother. Mother began whispering to her, murmuring something about counting days, bedding, a ritual bath.

The young man came in and said, "Well, my wife, let's go."

"Now you can reveal it: where are you taking me?"

"To the Hotel Krakowski."

"I'm not going to a hotel."

"Where are we going to sleep—in the street?"

"Let's go home."

"There are no more trains today."

Mother asked, "Do they have a mezuzah on the door?"

"For me today is like the night of Pesach. On Pesach the demons have no power," the young man declared. "Today we don't need a mezuzah." The young man pointed to his wife. "She's my little mezuzah!"

"Oh, he's crazy!"

"Rebbetzin, you don't know what I've gone through the past couple of years. We had a lessee who had a barn full of cows. A Jew came and bought a barren cow from him. The cow cried all the way home. It cried all day, it cried all night. This went on for two days, three days, a week. Rebbetzin, the cow cried until it died. It was longing for its mother or the other cows. The same thing happened to me. One day I divorced her and the next I began crying. The crying was within me, here, in my heart. I always thought I could damp the longing, make it mute, but it became worse and worse. If I hadn't returned and if we hadn't gotten married again, I would've ended up like that cow."

"And I—didn't I suffer plenty, too?"

The man took his wife and walked down the stairs with her. Outside, he waited for a droshky. He waved his parasol right and left. Finally, an empty droshky pulled up. The young man helped his wife get in, then he climbed up after her. He cast one last look at our balcony—the look of a man half crazy with love and impatience.

SHE SURELY

WILL BE ASHAMED

ოდ

In Father's courtroom all kinds of divorces took place, but this
one was different. The husband and wife loved each other; they
had lived together more than forty years. The husband was himself a rabbi. She was a rebbetzin. They had married children
and grandchildren. The couple exuded Torah learning and
familial lineage.

Why, then, did they want a divorce in their old age?

Because the husband, the rabbi, wanted to go to the Land of
Israel, but his wife, the rebbetzin, did not want to leave her children and grandchildren.

The rabbi could have left without getting a divorce, but the
fact of the matter is that a scholar cannot live by himself even in
the Land of Israel. A Jew must have a wife. He needs somebody
to cook him a warm meal, prepare his bed, send his clothes out
to be laundered, and darn his socks. Never mind how useful a
wife can be! The truth is that one is forbidden to be without a
wife because that can lead to impure thoughts and is an obstacle
to Torah study and prayer. A Jew who wants to lead a pure and

holy life has to have bread in his basket. In other words, he has to have a home and a wife.

The preparations to travel to the Land of Israel took years. A couple does not impetuously decide to divorce. But the rabbi was drawn to the Land of Israel as if by a magnet. For nights on end he could not sleep out of longing to be by the Western Wall; by the Cave of Machpela, where the patriarchs Abraham, Isaac, and Jacob are buried; by the tomb of Rachel in Bethlehem; and by other holy graves and ruins. He was also afraid that he might, God forbid, depart this world and lie buried in exile, in a land belonging to gentiles. The rebbetzin could under no circumstances decide to leave her family, so it gradually became clear that a divorce was the only way out.

The rabbi was apparently quite a bit older than the rebbetzin. His beard was as white as milk. He was dressed not like a rabbi but like a Hasidic rebbe: in a broad silk coat and shoes with white socks and a sable hat. For some time he had radiated the sanctity of the far-off places which he would visit. Father said that the rabbi was studying Kabbalah and assumed self-imposed fast days. When he stood to pray the Afternoon Service in our apartment, it took him exactly an hour to finish. He muttered, sighed, raised his hands up high. He pounded his chest as a Jew does on Yom Kippur when he recites the "For the sins that we have committed" prayer. He bent and bowed like Jews had once done in the Holy Temple. For supper he ate a piece of dried challah and drank a glass of curdled milk.

The rebbetzin had red cheeks, lively eyes, and a mouth that loved to nosh. She had arrived with a kerchief full of biscuits and candies on which she continually nibbled. She sat in our kitchen and said, "This isn't for me, Rebbetzin. I'm used to this place. I have my apartment, my bedding, my children and grandchildren, may they live to be one hundred and twenty years old. How could one leave all this behind? Sure, the Land of Israel is a holy land. When the Messiah comes, we will all be there, God willing . . ." The rebbetzin took out a handkerchief and blew her nose loudly.

"This is all rather strange," Mother said half to the rebbetzin and half to herself.

"Rebbetzin, he is a sage!" the woman said. "He is more in heaven than on earth. He was quite ready to go without a divorce, but I knew that he would suffer. Who would care for him there? He's the father of my children, may he live to be one hundred and twenty years old."

Mother sat silently. I saw on her face that she was angry at the rebbetzin. My mother felt that a wife must accompany her husband wherever he goes. All the more so when one has a husband like this one. The man was a saint! But what could be done? The rebbetzin had her own reasons. Just as part of her husband was in heaven, so she, the rebbetzin, stood with both her slippered feet on the ground. She loved her children with a passion. From time to time she stuck out the tip of her tongue and licked her lips. After a while she looked around to see how my mother kept house and I could tell by her expression that she was dissatisfied with my mother's domesticity.

While the scribe was writing the divorce document, and even before that, when the witnesses were being instructed how to affix their signatures, the rebbetzin spoke about fish, meat, fritters, beans, and pancakes. She gave my mother all kinds of advice regarding cooking and baking. The more the rebbetzin spoke, the clearer it became how earthbound she was, how deeply she was immersed in the pleasures of this world.

Mother nodded, but I saw that she had no patience for all this talk. Finally she broke in: "What's the point of being so occupied with eating?"

The rebbetzin looked askance. "If you're already eating, why shouldn't it taste good?" she asked.

"It has a good taste."

"I feel that if the dish is not prepared exactly as it should be, I can't put it in my mouth," the rebbetzin declared. "My mother, may she have a bright Paradise, would say, 'What one puts into the pot is what you take out. The pot cannot be fooled.'"

"It's better to fool the pot than oneself," my mother answered sharply.

In the other room sat the rabbi. He swayed back and forth, holding his high forehead, and for a while was lost in thought. The man was no longer here but somewhere in Jerusalem, in Safed, by the ruined synagogue of Rabbi Yehuda the Pious, by the grave of Rabbi Shimon Bar Yochai.

When it was time for the divorce, the rabbi placed the writ in the rebbetzin's hands and she wept. Then she said, "I did it for you so that you can go to the Land of Israel."

My father cast a glance into the holy text he was reading and addressed the rebbetzin: "If you want to get married, you must wait three months and a day."

The rebbetzin began crying once more. "May it happen to my enemies!"

"That is the law."

"I had one husband and one God . . ."

The rebbetzin left. Even the previous night she had slept at her daughter's house. The rabbi bade goodbye to Father. There was an oppressive heaviness in the house. Father paced back and forth. "No small thing, the Land of Israel! It is written that he who does not live in the Land of Israel is as if, God forbid, he had no Creator."

"Perhaps you'd like to go, too?" Mother asked.

"If only I could . . ."

"Why can't you? So many Jews are accepting charity there— so there will be one more."

"Well, well . . ."

"If you want a divorce, you can have one," Mother said with resentment.

"God forbid!"

Weddings brought a festive atmosphere into our apartment. Divorces left an emptiness. Mother went back to the kitchen and spoke to me as though I were a grownup. "What does she have to do here? Her children are already grown. They can live without their mother. Grandchildren can certainly survive without a grandmother. But she's afraid she's not going to have enough meat. It's the fleshpots of Egypt."

Many weeks passed. One day a letter arrived from the Land of Israel. The stamp was Turkish. Father carefully opened the envelope and removed a very small sheet of paper. The rabbi had written Father from Jerusalem, describing where he had been and what he had seen. He also included an original interpretation of a Talmudic passage. Father carried this piece of paper around; he read it once and then again. He said to me, "This little piece of paper has been in the Land of Israel."

"Very thin paper," I observed.

"Even objects become holy in the Land of Israel," Father declared. "They absorb its holiness."

"And what about mud?" I asked.

"Little silly. What is mud? Earth and water."

"And what about garbage?"

"What is garbage? The Almighty has created everything."

One day Father returned from the *shtibl* quite agitated. "Oh my, oh my!"

"What happened?" Mother asked. "Has the Radziminer Rebbe come up with another miracle?"

Father explained that the rabbi's wife had gotten married. She had found a wealthy older man.

"It can't be!"

"Mordecai the trustee himself told me."

Mother's thin lips began to move. I knew she was about to make a pointed, stinging remark, but instead she covered her mouth with her hand. "I'd better be quiet," she said, suppressing her desire to speak slander.

At a bris, where my father was given the honor of holding the baby during the ceremony, my mother met the former rebbetzin. No longer a rebbetzin, she had now become a businesswoman. She was adorned with lots of jewelry, which her new husband had given her, left over from his deceased wife. The former rebbetzin wanted to embrace my mother, but Mother retreated from her. The woman bragged about her beautiful apartment, which was full of carpets, silverware, dresses, and fur coats which her husband had made for her. She explained to Mother, "Rebbetzin, it's so hard to be alone. Children are children, but one must have a home. Being without one is like being lost at sea."

"Do you hear anything from him?" Mother asked.

"He writes very little."

"Has he married?"

"No."

"Why not?"

"Who knows. He's not a man, he's an angel." The woman bit into a big slice of honey cake and drank some sweet liqueur.

"May we continue to meet at happy occasions!" was her wish for Mother and herself, too.

More time passed. Father again returned from the Hasidic *shtibl* discomfited.

"What happened now?" Mother asked.

Father told us that the rabbi who had divorced his wife in our apartment had died.

"Was he sick?"

"Who knows!"

Mother lowered her head. It's an old story: the gluttons, the guzzlers, the swindlers, the thieves live long lives. The righteous ones die before their time—but why should this be so? Well, one can't ask questions of the Master of the Universe.

Father said, "He was buried last Friday. He won't have to undergo the suffering in the grave."

Father and I went into the study. "What is this world of ours? The years fly by. How long has it been since I was a little boy? It seems only yesterday. Man takes nothing with him except Torah and good deeds."

"Will the rabbi be in Paradise?" I asked.

"That's some question you're asking!"

"And will the rebbetzin go to hell?"

"God forbid. Why should she? . . . But you should know that even Paradise has various levels." Father spoke at length with me about the sanctity of the Land of Israel. He said that according to the law, we are all impure, but the Almighty above has compassion upon us—for it's not the poor Jews' fault. Our exile is as long as the night, but salvation will come, it will come.

"When, Father?"

"When we are worthy."

"When?"

"It depends on you."

"On me?"

"Yes, on you and me, and every Jew individually. The poor Messiah is pleading that he wants to come, but he's not allowed to because Jews are sinful. Repent, and the Messiah will come!"

The former rebbetzin lived another couple of years; then she, too, died. People discussed this in the Radziminer *shtibl.* I thought that the woman would certainly be ashamed to appear in the world to come. What would she say to her ex-husband, that righteous man? Wouldn't she be ashamed to stand in his presence?

HE WANTS FORGIVENESS
FROM HER

ᔕᓚ

The door opened and into the room came a fashionable, beard-less young man wearing a stovepipe hat and a short jacket. He seemed to be in his late thirties. His appearance and manner of dress, indeed his entire bearing, radiated importance — that of a doctor, a lawyer, or, at the very least, an accountant. Especially authoritative were his pince-nez, which sat low down on his nose and were fastened to the buttonhole in his lapel by a thin black cord.

"Well, what's the good word?" my father said.

The young man spoke half shyly and hesitantly. He began with these words: "Rabbi, you're going to laugh . . ."

It turned out that some twelve years before, the young man had been the fiancé of a respectable Warsaw girl. Then he met an-other girl and married her. People warned him that when some-one breaks off an engagement, a letter of forgiveness is required from the other party. But he was in love with his new wife and was ashamed to return to the first one to request the letter. He was especially ashamed before his in-laws. In short, he went off to live with the second girl, moved to another city, and hoped that time would smooth everything over. So a match dissolves, big deal!

However, bad luck tagged after the young man. He opened a shop, but it failed. He established a factory: that, too, did not succeed. His wife had one child, a second child, a third child, but all of them died. The young man was not religious; still, these misfortunes reminded him of the wrong that he had done to his first fiancée. He began to ponder this, and started dreaming about it at night. Before long he became obsessed with the thought that he would have no respite until he got a pardon from his former fiancée, who he heard had married. The news prompted him to leave his business and come to Warsaw, where he discovered that his former fiancée lived in our—that is my father's—district. That is why he had come to ask my father's assistance in getting a letter of forgiveness.

Father heard him out before saying, "Yes, it's true. When a person is wronged, repentance is of no avail. One must request forgiveness."

Father then sent me to bring the man's former fiancée to the courtroom.

Since she lived on Khlodna Street, the young man gave me money for the round trip on the droshky. It was weird sitting in a droshky without packages. The boys outside gaped in wonder. The shopkeepers, men and women, laughed and wagged a warning forefinger at me. I leaned my head against the side of the droshky and felt the springs swaying under me. I was so light I was afraid I might fall out. Nevertheless, I felt comfortable riding in the droshky. I closed my eyes and contemplated the strangeness of human relationships. Because a young man in Lodz or Kolish can't sleep at night for thinking about his former fiancée, I, a young boy from Krochmalna Street, have to be in a droshky on a Wednesday noon.

I passed through the elegant gate of the woman's building, climbed up a marble staircase to her apartment, and rang the bell. A maid clad in a white apron opened the door and asked me what I wanted.

"The lady of the house is being called to the rabbi's courtroom."

The woman soon appeared. She was in her late thirties, still pretty, but her high bosom was heavy, and she had scattered strands of gray hair. She looked as imposing in her womanliness as did her former fiancé in his manliness. She asked me why I had come.

"Your former fiancé is summoning you to see the rabbi—my father," I said.

The woman's big dark eyes widened. "What fiancé? And what rabbi?"

As I told the woman everything I had heard, I noticed the color changing on her face—now pale, now red. One moment she was about to burst into laughter, the next she turned sad. At one point I thought she was going to yell at me and drive me from the apartment. Then she seemed to soften. "Do you already understand these matters?" she asked.

"I understand everything," I said with boyish boastfulness.

"Wait. I'm going to phone my husband."

After I had waited for a long time in the corridor, the young woman came out wearing a coat and hat.

"Let's go."

I told her I had money for a droshky, but she said she'd pay for the droshky herself. Soon I was sitting next to her—a lady from Khlodna Street going to meet her former fiancé, accompanied by a boy with red sidecurls, who knew bizarre secrets, was mixed up in the affairs of strangers, and was thinking wild thoughts. The woman herself did not interest me that much, but I couldn't take my eyes off the horse. I sat to the side, where I could observe the horse's broad hindquarters and long tail, which swayed and seemed to tell me mutely: I don't care who I carry or where I go. I don't know anything. I'm a horse's rear and I'll always be one. When I eat oats, I have the strength to pull this droshky. I don't care whether a priest, a rabbi, or a Turk is sitting in it. From time to time the horse's tail swished, a sign that its hindquarters were satisfied.

As I climbed the stairs to our apartment with the woman, I noticed that her dress was narrow and long. She had to take small steps and was unable to negotiate two stairs at a time. The heels of her shoes were high and shiny. Pharmacy fragrances clung to her. She took me by the sleeve, as if to lean on me for protection. Her gloved hand was both light and firm. A strange, forbidden warmth ran through me, which turned me into an absolute ass.

The meeting between the once-engaged couple was like something out of a fairy tale. It also reminded me of the story of Joseph and his brothers. The man didn't recognize the woman at first. They looked at each other in amazement, alternating between forgetfulness and remembrance. Finally, the woman declared, "Yes, it's you."

"I recognized you right away," the man said, intending it as a compliment.

"How long has it been? No, better don't tell me," the woman said.

"How the years fly by!"

"When did you start wearing glasses?"

"About three years ago. Maybe four."

"Are you nearsighted, or what?"

"Yes."

"I've become fat."

While they were exchanging these banalities, Father perused a holy text, stroking his beard and rubbing his forehead. Just as I had been totally absorbed in the horse's hindquarters before, I was now all eyes and ears regarding this couple who had almost become man and wife but had become estranged on account of a love affair. Both of them now had someone else, yet a closeness remained. They addressed each other in the familiar form. They stood face-to-face and couldn't get their fill of looking at each other.

"What kind of man is your husband?" I heard him ask.

"A good man."

"Are you happy with him?"

"One can't always be happy," she replied.

"Fania," he said, "I've never forgotten the wrong I did."

And his glasses clouded over as if someone had breathed a mouthful of vapor on them.

The woman did not reply at once. Her face began to twitch. I saw a mist in her eyes which might become a tear, but, too proud after twelve years to cry in his presence, she held it back.

She raised her head. "I've already forgotten everything."

"Fania, God has punished me on account of you."

"How can you say that? One can never be sure of such things."

They talk; they murmur. Father waits, but he's impatient. The talking and murmuring of this formerly engaged couple smacks of sin.

"You're a married woman," Father tells her. "And he, too, has a family. Give him forgiveness and the One Above will help both of you."

"I forgive him," the woman declares. "And God will surely forgive him."

"It's preferable for the forgiveness to be in writing," Father says.

The word "forgiveness" makes me want to laugh. In Yiddish that word—*mekhila*—also has another meaning, and not a nice one: "rear end." I want to burst out laughing like a little boy, but I restrain myself with all my might. Father writes a few words in Hebrew. He makes two copies. The man has to give her a declaration of forgiveness and she has to give one to him—and both have to sign them.

"I can sign only in Polish," says the woman.

"All right, as long as it's signed," Father says.

She takes the pen in a grandiose manner, rests her finger on the holder, and, without removing her chamois glove, signs in a quavering calligraphy with her present husband's last name. Her signature evinces education, wealth, and worldliness. Only people who live on Khlodna Street and have a marble entrance staircase and a bell on the door have signatures like this. The man writes his name in Yiddish, but his signature, too, has a modern flourish.

"What's your name?" Father asks. "I can't make it out."

"Zigmunt."

"How are you called up to the Torah?"

"To the Torah? . . . Zalman."

"Sign again," Father orders. "With your Hebrew name."

The young man signs "Zalman."

Father gets a ruble and I have a forty-kopeck coin in my pocket. The couple leaves the apartment together. It seems to me that Father wants to call them back and warn them that they are not allowed to go together, but before he can say a word, they are already on their way downstairs.

I run out to the balcony, waiting to see them emerge from the front gate. But it takes a long time and I don't know what to think. Did they remain in the courtyard? Are they inside the gate? Or perhaps I missed them and they have already gone. I'm very impatient. Finally, they appear and he seems to be holding her by the arm. Not actually holding her, but supporting her elbow with his hand. Strange, how slowly they're moving. They stop repeatedly. They go not toward Khlodna Street but toward Gnoyna. They're so deep in conversation that they clearly don't even know where they're going.

I have already read the romances of the popular Yiddish writer Shomer, and my imagination is working overtime. Perhaps, I think, the man wants to take her to his castle. Perhaps he is a count. Perhaps she, the woman with him, is in disguise. Perhaps he will shoot her with a pistol and then take his own life. Perhaps the entire matter of forgiveness is only a ruse. Perhaps I should run down to the street and follow them. But no—they would recognize me. I remember the money in my pocket and decide to go to Tvarda Street to buy myself a story-book. Not one, but two. Not two, but six.

I run to Tvarda Street. The news vendor stands there wearing a little red cap. His small book rack is packed with books: Sherlock Holmes, Max Shpitzkopf, and titles like *Terrible Secrets, The Secret of the Kaiser's Court, the Captive Princess, The Enchanted Orphan Girl, The 1,200 Thieves*. Each title pulls me like a magnet. Each booklet has its own mystery, cleverness, and bizarre intrigues. But I can't buy them all. I have to choose.

I spend my last kopeck and carry home a stack of books. The street and the boys no longer concern me at all. I have only one wish: that my joy not be interrupted, that I have the time to read everything from beginning to end.

And at some point I muse that I, too, would like to write a storybook—full of secrets and mysteries, full of counts and orphan girls and enchanted thieves, starring a bride and groom named Fania and Zigmunt who haven't seen each other for twelve years and who then meet at a rabbi's house, whereupon their love is rekindled and begins to burn like a hellish fire.

A HASIDIC REBBE
ON THE STREET

ᜰᜰ

A Hasidic rebbe, whom I portrayed in my book *In My Father's
Court*, lived on our street. But one day a new rebbe moved in.
While the first was a grandson of the Kozhenitzer Rebbe, this
one, from the provinces, was connected to the Kotzk court and
related to the Rebbe of Kotzk's family.

The new rebbe had come to pay my father a visit. Short,
young, with a little blond beard, he wore a tattered silk gaberdine and a shabby high fur hat.

The fact that this new rebbe had moved to a street where a
rebbe already lived was considered an improper act of competi-
tion. But where should a rebbe live? There was no need for them
in the gentile quarter, and a Hasidic rebbe had already established his residence on the Jewish street.

The other Hasidic rebbe was already old, eighty or more.
What did an old man need? But the new rebbe had a young wife
and a houseful of children: girls with braids and boys with sidecurls down to their shoulders. Unlike the old rebbe, the new
one was a scholar. He could have been a rebbe with a court of

followers, but where could one find Hasidim for so many rebbes? So he just remained what people called a "grandson" or a "descendant" of a noted rebbe.

To succeed in a trade one must have luck, but it was immediately apparent that the young rebbe had no *mazel.* He looked too refined, too wise, too aristocratic for the simple women on the street. No one came to him. No one believed that he could intervene with God on their behalf. The old rebbe, then, had nothing to fear: the new one took no one away from him.

The new rebbe wanted me to befriend his little boys, and I went to play with them. The rooms in the apartment were half empty. A young woman, her head covered with a silk kerchief, was puttering around in the kitchen. The little girls were teaching each other the *aleph-beys* and copying lines of Hebrew script from a penmanship manual. The boys were swaying over Talmuds. Everything was fine and orderly in the apartment, but no one visited. No one knocked on the door. When someone *did* knock, it was a beggar going from door to door. The rebbetzin gave him a groschen or a piece of sugar.

The rebbe, who had a pale face, blue eyes, and a high forehead, wandered about the apartment in a silk robe. He had all the attributes of a Hasidic rebbe: fine familial lineage, scholarly ability, a talent for preaching and sharing the bread at his table, and perhaps even for producing a miraculous feat. But no one needed him. All the bankruptcy of the Hasidic courts radiated out of him.

One day the rebbe came to talk to Father. Sitting at the table, he said, "The Jews in your street have no regard for me."

"They don't come to you?"

"They don't even stick their nose in the door."

"They don't need us," Father said in sympathy, using the plural.

"The waters have risen up to here," the rebbe said, quoting the psalms, pointing to his thin throat, long and white as a girl's.

"Can I help you in any way?" Father asked.

"No, no."

Mother brought in the usual glass of tea and Sabbath biscuits. The rebbe held the glass with long, thin fingers. He looked at Mother with his kindly Jewish eyes, which seemed to say, Look what's become of us . . .

Suddenly the rebbe declared, "Rabbi, I'm going to America."

Father looked confused. "To America?"

"Yes. America."

"What will you do in America?"

"I'm going to rid myself of humiliation. I'm going to become a tailor."

Father seemed embarrassed by these words. "Some fine tailor!"

The rebbe took hold of his beard. "What do you think? Will I be a good tailor? In America one doesn't have to sew an entire garment. It's enough if you sew on a button or a loop."

"It's not for you. Not for you."

"And is starving with my family any better? 'Rather skin a carcass in the market,' says the Talmud, 'than depend on charity.'"

"Still . . . what about your children?"

"One can also be a Jew in America."

"Yes, but . . ."

"In America, people walk around upside down," I called out.

Father cast a rather angry glance at me. "You're talking nonsense."

"But I read it in *The Book of the Covenant*."*

"You read, but you didn't understand," the rebbe said. He explained that people everywhere walk with their heads up and their feet on the ground. But pertaining to heavenly bodies, one cannot say precisely what is up and what is down. It was clear from the rebbe's words that he had dipped into secular books.

Then Father asked, "Well . . . do you know any foreign languages?"

"I know Russian, Polish, and German, too."

"How?"

"I looked into books."

"Hmmm . . . it's not a good situation."

The rebbe kept his word. I don't know how, but he obtained passage for his entire family. A little sign that had hung on the gate stating that the rebbe lived there had been removed. I witnessed a quiet revolution at his house. The rebbetzin removed her silk kerchief and donned a wig. The boys' sidecurls were shortened. The rebbe had discarded his silk gaberdine and now wore a ribbed cotton cloak. It was clear that he was not going to America to be a rebbe but would indeed learn tailoring.

* *The Book of the Covenant,* a traditional book popular at the end of the eighteenth century that dealt with various aspects of science and philosophy.

Once, when I went to his house, I saw him reading a newspaper. He even peeked into a novel. It seemed as if he were saying silently: Since God doesn't need me, I don't need Him. The boys ran about, yelling and fooling around, and their father let them. It was strange, but the rebbe's appearance had changed—he looked stronger and more manly. Now he discussed mundane matters with his wife. Then someone knocked on the door and I watched a bizarre scene unfold.

A woman came in and asked, "Does the rebbe live here?"

The rebbetzin asked her what she wanted.

"Alas, my child is very ill!" the woman began crying and wringing her hands.

Instead of her being escorted to the rebbe's study, the rebbe came to see her in the kitchen. He asked her what ailed the child. When she replied, the rebbe said, "Why have you come to me? Go to a doctor."

"Holy rabbi, first God and then you."

"I can't help you in any way," the rebbe said.

"Holy saint!"

"I am not a saint. I'm a plain Jew."

"Aren't you the rebbe?" The woman stopped crying for a moment.

"I'm a rebbe no longer!"

The woman wanted to give the rebbe a gulden, but he refused to take it, saying, "Take the gulden, see a doctor, and buy medicine."

Just then the youngest boy whispered into my ear: "In America I'm going to cut off my sidecurls."

"Will your father let you?"

"He himself said so. He's also going to send me to public school."

"To public school?"

"Yes . . . public school."

The rebbe wasn't merely emigrating to America, he was conducting a strike against God. His face expressed rebelliousness and impatience. The look in the rebbetzin's eyes seemed to radiate hatred. And strangely, the rebbe never even came to bid farewell to Father.

Sad news concerning the rebbe soon made its way to us. Someone reported that he had seen the family at the Vienna train station. The rebbetzin was wearing a hat. The boys' side-curls had been cut off. The rebbe wore Western-style clothes and a fedora in the German fashion.

For a while we heard nothing more and then someone from Brussels wrote a letter to a relative in Warsaw stating that he had met the family there. One of the rebbe's daughters had had an eye problem which needed treatment. The rebbe had eaten in a restaurant that was not glatt kosher, a place where truly pious Jews would not even set foot.

More time passed with no news of the rebbe. Then one of the Jews on our street got a letter from his brother in New York saying that the rebbe was working alongside him in the same shop. He had shaved off his beard. He worked all day long standing next to gentile girls.

Every fresh bit of news was a blow to Father, but he did not get angry. True, one could not wage war against the Almighty, and this rebbe was not conducting himself properly. Nevertheless, sometimes one has to address God with a sharp word. He shouldn't assume that He can do what He wishes to Jews and they will routinely stretch their necks out for slaughter. If He wants Jews, He should provide them with a livelihood. If He wants Torah and Yiddishkeit, He should see to it that they are held in high regard.

In fact, while Father didn't articulate this, one could see in his eyes something akin to triumph mingled with sorrow. It seemed to me that Father's thoughts went something like this: If such a fine young man from such a glorious family lineage could abandon the straight and narrow path, it would be noted in heaven that the situation of the Jews was critical and that the Messiah would have to come.

I, too, was pleased with this news. It showed that everything was falling apart. Who knows? Perhaps they would also let me cut off my sidecurls. Perhaps Father, too, would go to America. I had a strong desire to go somewhere—every time I heard a train whistle, the longing was reawakened. In my fantasy I saw the rebbe in a factory, bareheaded, clean-shaven, a gentile girl on either side of him. The rebbe was sewing buttons, singing a song like the ones the journeymen sang in their workshops. The rebbetzin's hair was not covered. Their sons, my friends, went to public school and wrote on the Sabbath. Who knows, perhaps they even ate unkosher food. I fancied that when the rebbe came home from work, the rebbetzin told him, Today I cooked noodles and ham . . .

A year or more must have passed. Then out of the blue we got a letter from the rebbe declaring that it had indeed been his ambition to be a worker. For a long time he had slaved away at the factory, but he didn't have the strength for it. Then someone suggested that he study slaughtering. The rebbe wrote to Father asking him to send him the slaughterer's handbook, *Tevuos Shor.*

The letter pleased Father and he showed it to the men in the Hasidic *shtibl.* "See, he's a scion of the pious, after all," he said.

But I didn't take kindly to that sort of submissiveness. I wanted the rebbe to convert. I wanted his boys to become Christians. I was overflowing with modern rebelliousness and a mad desire for upheaval, extraordinary news, weird changes. I dreamed that the moon had fallen, the sun was extinguished, an earthquake had rocked Warsaw—even that the hill in Krashinsky Park suddenly started to spew fire and become what *The Book of the Covenant* called a volcano.

"Papa, how would you look without a beard?" I once asked Father.

Father cast a frightened look at me. "Don't talk nonsense!"

I imagined Father without a beard, without a mustache, and wearing a straw hat, checkered trousers, and yellow shoes. I began laughing and crying at once. A pair of scissors or a razor could have made Father beardless. Just trimming down Father's gaberdine would make him look fashionably German. He, too, could have been placed among gentile girls and been told to sew buttons . . . Suddenly I took hold of Father's beard and tugged it.

"What are you doing, you rascal!" Father scolded me good-naturedly.

A horrible thought took hold of me: he could have been converted, too, God forbid . . . Father could have become a gentile. A cold chill ran through me and a lump knotted my throat. Anything could happen to a human being. A man could even be slaughtered like an animal and his flesh chopped on a butcher block.

"Why are you looking at me like that? What are you thinking? Why aren't you studying?" Father asked me.

I kissed Father on the forehead. "Stay the way you are!"

THE TINSMITH
AND THE HOUSEMAID

ℭℭ

One sees all kinds of unhappy people in the course of one's life, but the young couple I will now depict were unhappy in an unusual way. It wasn't until years later that I began to understand what had happened.

It began with the couple getting married in our apartment. Since both were short, they looked younger than they really were. He was a tinsmith, and she had once been a housemaid. He was swarthy, Oriental-looking, and prematurely balding, with a high forehead. His coal-black eyes had a strange glow. I had seen him several times clambering barefoot on slanty rooftops with feline agility.

The woman was broad-set, with a big shock of wiry hair, a flat nose, and thick lips. For many years she had worked as a maid, had assembled a trousseau, and had saved up money for a dowry. The two met and married immediately. Both were orphans.

Husband and wife rented a fairly nice apartment, which they furnished. He worked for a master tinsmith, and she, his young wife, was now the mistress of the household and went to market with her basket. For the first couple of weeks it seemed that everything was going well.

Then an argument broke out. The wife came to us to complain that her husband constantly grumbled, picked on her, and reproached her. She didn't speak with Father but with Mother.

"What does he want from you?" Mother asked.

"Rebbetzin, I don't know. I give him a plate of food straight from the fire and he shouts that it's cold. Here he says I've oversalted the food and there he says it has no salt at all. The soup is too watery, the meat is too hard, the milk is curdled. He interferes in my household affairs, too. I have to account to him for every penny, and if a penny is missing, he makes such a fuss that all the neighbors hear it."

"Has he always been so stingy?"

"No. When he was engaged to me, he threw money around. I would have to restrain him not to spend so much."

"Perhaps he's angry about something."

"Why should he be angry? I haven't caused him any harm . . ."

"Perhaps his boss is giving him trouble?"

"No."

"Perhaps he's not well."

"I haven't got the faintest idea."

Mother gave the woman the eternal womanly advice: Wait, have patience, sometimes a crazy notion gets into a man's head. Sometimes a man suffers but doesn't want to talk about it—so he takes it out on his wife. What can one do? One must put up with everything. With time, when a man sees that his wife is loyal and devoted to him, he becomes nice and stays that way.

This is what Mother said. I heard her advice and was pleased that she spoke with such respect about men. When I grew up, I too would become a man . . .

The woman left, apparently ready to obey Mother.

But instead of being good and submissive, the woman drank half a bottle of essence of vinegar after their next argument, then ran at once to a neighbor's apartment with burned lips, groaning, "Help me!"

They called out the rescue-squad wagon and the attendants pumped the woman's stomach.

A couple of weeks later a fire broke out in their apartment. The woman opened the window that faced the courtyard and shouted, "Help! Fire!"

Someone telephoned the fire department, and they came at once with their wild horses. First the firemen smashed all the windows in the apartment, then they broke the new furniture, and only then did they extinguish the flames. The fire itself was a mystery. The woman said that she had opened her clothes closet and a fire ensued.

"How do you get flames in a clothes closet?" her neighbors wanted to know.

"I ask you!" she replied.

Some time passed. Then one day the street suddenly turned black with people. The young tinsmith had fallen off a roof. He wasn't killed, but he had broken a leg. His fall was also a mystery—the roof was less steep than others and he had been standing next to the chimney. There had been no wind. In the hospital, he told people who had come to visit him to learn what had happened that he felt as if two hands had seized him by the shoulders and pushed him. He had tried to hold on to the roof's gutters, but that other, the one who had pushed him, was stronger than he.

"Wait a minute. Who was pushing you?"

"It must've been a demon."

"In the middle of the day?"

"Well, you see what happened."

People could not understand. On the other hand, on occasion tinsmiths fall from roofs. That business with the hands was probably his imagination. But clearly ill luck was plaguing the couple.

Soon the tinsmith left the hospital and the woman became pregnant. It seemed that everything was now going smoothly. But then the woman had a miscarriage. She declared that she was standing in the kitchen, cooking soup, when the door suddenly opened and a black cat ran in. Her sudden fright caused hemorrhaging.

"Perhaps the door was open," someone suggested.

"No. It was shut. Someone turned the handle and let the cat in."

"Who could that have been?"

"I know like you know."

People on the street began saying all kinds of things. Some said that the misfortunes were occurring because the woman had the same name as her husband's mother. Others suspected that she wasn't heeding carefully the laws of family purity and wasn't going to the ritual bath at the proper time. Father told a scribe to inspect the mezuzahs. He also lent the couple a volume of the Zohar, which was considered a charm to drive demons from one's house.

For a while it was quiet. Then, one Friday night, the woman ate a chicken head and the beak got stuck either in her gullet or in her windpipe. Cries for help broke out in the courtyard. Once again the rescue squad was called and a doctor removed the chicken head from the woman's throat. The doctor declared that had he arrived ten minutes later he wouldn't have found her alive.

One misfortune came on the heels of another. The courtyard gaped and was astounded. It was obvious that something was amiss. Evil powers had besieged the couple. But why them?

There was another round of fires. Not great conflagrations but smaller fires. A garbage container burst into flames all by itself and flickered with a hellish fire. The woman quickly doused it with a pitcher of water. Two hours later, when she went into her bedroom, she saw a little flame bouncing around the bedcover, which she smothered with a jacket. A day or two later, a curtain caught fire and burned.

Each time the woman came running to my father, but Father told her to see a Hasidic rebbe. Such things were not his specialty. She needed a Hasidic master who could give her amulets, pieces of amber over which spells were cast, or other charms to drive away demons. During those years great rebbes did not yet live in Warsaw (they started arriving only after World War I). The woman went off to see a small-time rebbe. He told her to place pieces of garlic on the walls, a remedy against ghosts and imps. The woman bought a wreath of garlic and placed cloves on all the walls. But they did not help.

Once, while she was scraping the scales off a fish, a scale slid under her nail. Her finger swelled up and she developed a high fever. Gangrene almost set in, but a doctor performed a minor operation, after which her hand began improving. I don't remember all the misfortunes that plagued that house. I only remember that one trouble followed another; however, they never suffered a full-fledged tragedy. It seemed that the dark powers wanted to frighten them more than kill them.

During those years a famous fortune-teller and reader of cards named Schiller Shkolnick lived in Warsaw. He placed advertisements in newspapers stating that he gave advice and could read cards, could find stolen goods or lost relatives. It was said that he had a black mirror hanging in a dark room in which a deserted wife could find her vanished husband. My father told the woman that she was forbidden to go to him because his deeds smacked of magic, pagan customs, and the black arts of the nations who had lived in the Land of Israel before Jews had conquered it. But neighbors convinced the woman that Schiller Shkolnick was the only one who could help her.

Supposedly, when she went to see Schiller Shkolnick, he wrote all sorts of charms and told her all kinds of things. But precisely what he did and said I don't know. I only remember people saying that he, the famous Schiller Shkolnick, could not help either.

After that the husband and wife came to Father and asked him to divorce them. Father never rushed through with a divorce. He advised them to move out of their apartment.

"The Talmud teaches that he who changes his place changes his luck," he declared. "It happens that sometimes an apartment is unlucky. There's always time to get a divorce."

Apparently the couple was not too anxious to divorce. They moved out of the apartment and found a new one somewhere in the fancier district, either on Mizke Street or on Mila Lane.

Strangely, this simple remedy helped. We began hearing good news about them. Their troubles had ceased. The woman became pregnant again. The tinsmith found work with another master.

The landlord of the previous apartment house was angry at Father. For several months the apartment remained empty. Finally, a gentile moved in. It seemed that the spirits had a score to settle only with that couple—the goy they left alone.

The master tinsmith came to visit us once in a while, and he often spoke about the couple. They had stopped arguing and now they lived like a pair of doves. The woman completed her pregnancy and gave birth to a boy. She was terrified before her lying-in, because it was known that demons have power over a woman in labor. But everything went well. The child was healthy. Now everything was fine and dandy with them.

I said earlier that only lately have I begun to understand what happened with that couple. But I'm still not sure that I really understand it.

A Freudian might interpret all of this as follows: The husband and wife subconsciously tried to sabotage their life together. Perhaps he or she had another love. Perhaps they weren't happy sexually. It is easy to hang the blame for everything on sex and the subconscious.

One might also say that the couple was the victim of a poltergeist, the same sort of spirit which several months ago emptied bottles of liquid in a house on Long Island and threw things with an invisible hand. But what is a poltergeist? And why did he beset that particular apartment? This belongs to that category of things where the facts are known but no cogent explanation for them exists. Yes, it is connected with a person's spiritual attitude. That much is certain. Our inner attitude and outer circumstances are closely bound together. But what sort of connection exists and how it operates—that has not yet been discovered. Only during the past few years have people come to realize that such a link does indeed exist.

WHAT'S THE PURPOSE
OF SUCH A LIFE?

ಬಿ

Those who understand human nature and contemplate its affairs realize that one person can never really know another. People do things which seem to make no sense at all.

For example. the middle-aged man who married a woman fifteen years younger and then began to work as a salesman, traveling the length and breadth of Russia to sell the products of a big firm on commission. He got married, let's say on a Tuesday, and then on Sunday, even before the traditional seven days of celebration had ended, his wife was accompanying him to the train bound for Petersburg. He had planned to be away three months, but ended up traversing all of Russia up to the Chinese border and didn't return until seven months later.

He remained in Warsaw three weeks and then departed once more. When he came back again, the traveling salesman found a baby in a cradle—his own.

I won't recount all his trips here. At the lawsuit his wife listed each one in detail. He had been at home no more than one month during the year and sometimes not even that long. Another child was born. The children were already seven and eight, but they did not really know their father. He came, brought presents, and once more began preparing for another journey. After each trip he would promise his wife that his roaming and roving had ended, but he never kept his word.

He looked like a traveling salesman: average height, rather chubby, with a black mustache and the smile of a peddler. He had a premature potbelly on which hung the gold chain of a pocketwatch. He dressed fashionably: a derby, a pinstriped suit, a stiff collar with rounded edges, and a black necktie. His boots were polished to a high shine. Even the way he inserted a finger into his vest pocket and lit his cigarettes with a lighter proved he was a worldly man.

He said in a pleasantly hoarse voice, "Is it my fault I have such a livelihood? This is how I make my living. This is how I support my family."

The way he blew smoke rings through his nose and from the side of his mouth showed me, the little boy, that he was full of grown-up cleverness and that he knew what he was talking about.

But above all, I liked his cuffs with the gilt cuff links set with blue gemstones. A man with such cuffs just doesn't babble aimlessly.

But his short wife, who had a girlish face and wore a hat over her head of girlish hair, countered, "What kind of a living is this? He goes away for years on end. I'm a living widow and the children are living orphans. On Pesach I have to go to my mother's for the Seder . . ." The woman took out a small handkerchief and wiped away a solitary tear.

Father placed his hand on his forehead and asked, "So what do you want?"

"Rather than live such a life, it would be better for him to divorce me," the woman said. "I can't go on like this. It's a miserable way to live."

"What do you say?" Father asked the husband.

"Rabbi, if she wants to divorce me, I won't force her to stay. My principle is that two people have to want a marriage. If one side is dissatisfied, it's no good."

The word "marriage" smacked of storybooks and novels serialized in the newspapers. Even the word "dissatisfied" had a Germanic ring.

Mother came in and asked, "What's the purpose of such a life?"

She said it partly to the woman and partly to the man. The traveling salesman smiled sweetly, displaying some of the gold in his teeth. His words, too, were golden: "What shall I do, Rebbetzin? Every person has his occupation. Do you think it's a pleasure to sit days on end in a train? One day I'm in Moscow, the next I'm in Petersburg; one day I'm in Nizhny Novgorod, and the next I'm in Vladivostok. And furthermore, living in hotels is no pleasure either. I long for my own bed and my wife. But no sooner do I want to return home than I get a telegram from my firm to go to the Caucasus, or the devil knows where. Then I have to pick up my suitcase and run to the terminal once again . . ."

"Children must have a father . . ."

"Of course, but my situation is such that I can see my children only once a year."

I was only a little boy at the time, but still I sensed that this man was not as unhappy as he pretended to be. A joke always seemed to hover on his thick lips. He apparently enjoyed these trips immensely. His eyes gleamed with oily satisfaction and pride that he was needed by his firm and was obliged to undertake such lengthy journeys. It seemed he felt quite at home in all these trains, terminals, hotels. By now I had already heard readings of the Sholom Aleichem railroad story about two traveling salesmen who played cards on the backside of a Greek Orthodox priest—and it seemed to me that this traveling salesman was one of those two men. He sits in the train, drinks tea, plays cards, and tells stories. Who knows what could have taken place in all those far-flung places?

After lengthy discussions the traveling salesman promised that he would try to persuade his firm to have him travel less and do more work in Warsaw. He took his wife by the arm and departed with her. Even his manner of walking was sly and deceitful. I noticed that two round pieces of rubber had been added to his heels to make him taller. One could not hear his footfalls. I sensed (or perhaps I realize it only now) that his wife and children were no more than a joke for him—one of the countless comic and entertaining anecdotes which traveling salesmen tell on trains to one another or to perfect strangers.

After a period of not going to the cheder, I was enrolled by my parents once again. It so happened that this was the same cheder that the older son of the traveling salesman was attending. He did not study with my teacher, who taught Talmud, but with the teacher's son, who taught the beginners' class. The boy had a gentile first name: Kuba. He attended cheder for only a few hours, because he also studied in public school. He came and went as he wished. The boy was a copy of his father: chubby, swarthy, with a pair of dark, laughing eyes, full lips, and dimpled cheeks. His pockets were always laden with nuts, chocolates, caramels, and all kinds of toys. Despite his age he was full of stories. He didn't know that his parents had come to us to initiate a lawsuit, but I *did* know and played dumb. Children often have a good sense of what can be discussed and what must be kept secret. I already knew not to tell tales out of school . . .

Kuba was always blathering about his papa: how he traveled, how he saw everything, and what kinds of presents he brought every time he returned home. The boy had a set of trains with tracks and other such toys. Even the trifles he brought to cheder were treasures. He had, for example, an ivory pen whose shaft had a tiny window. Looking into it one could see the city of Cracow. He also had colored pencils and even a little box of colors with which one could paint only when they were wet with spittle.

At some point, a week passed and the would-be scholar (which is what the teacher called him) did not show up in cheder. The teacher then sent me and another boy to find out what had happened. Perhaps Kuba was ill.

We made our way to their house. The family no longer lived on our street but on Gnoyna Street. The apartment steps were dirty, but underneath the dirt one could see the white of marble. I rang the bell and a maid came to open the door. At first she didn't want to admit us, but Kuba heard us and invited us in. I stood there amazed. The rooms were enormous. Kuba was wearing something I hadn't seen before; only later did I learn it was pajamas. He was supposedly a little bit under the weather. His throat was red, but he played with his toys and ran about over the waxed floors with the energy of a young colt. His mother yelled at him and the maid scolded him angrily in Polish.

Suddenly I noticed a man roaming about the house, but it wasn't the traveling salesman. He was short, thin, with a pale face and blond curly hair. His tie looked more like a noose than a cravat. I asked Kuba who he was.

"He's teaching Mama how to play the piano."

"What's that?"

"Come, I'll show you."

He ran to the piano and began banging on the keys. Tones and overtones filled the apartment. His mother began yelling at Kuba in Polish, and we, the two messengers, wanted to leave, but then she offered us a snack. Each one of us was given a biscuit and a glass of cocoa, as was Kuba, but he was in no rush to drink. He was already sated with sweets.

Kuba told us about the piano teacher. He could play anything. He was a professor of music and had performed with the Philharmonic. He was also crazy. When Mama did not play well, he plugged his ears with his fingers and yelled and swooshed the sheet music to the floor. Sometimes the teacher took Kuba and his little sister, who was now at school, to the movies, where they showed all kinds of little people on a screen. The piano teacher did not speak Yiddish, only Polish.

"Is he your uncle?"

"No, he's not an uncle."

I wasn't suspicious at the time, but I understood that none of this was kosher. All these things smacked of promiscuity: a piano, a woman without a marriage wig, a man who gave piano lessons to a woman, a little boy who studied in public school and ran around bareheaded in the apartment. I never saw him again—not him, not his mama, not the piano teacher, and not his father, who dragged himself from one Russian fair to another and supported a nice-looking wife, two refined children, and a piano teacher to boot.

This traveling salesman who told countless anecdotes about others had transformed his own life into an anecdote. But why did he do this? Why did a man get married and then go off to faraway places? Did he have such strong faith in women's fidelity? Or didn't it bother him? And why did he need a family whom he saw so rarely?

A stranger certainly cannot answer this, but I don't know if even the salesman himself could have explained it. Behind his jokes and tales a different being evidently lived in this man—one with another outlook and other calculations.

A LAWSUIT AND A DIVORCE

ᘛᙚ

I'll admit to you, dear reader, that I don't care much for dogs. The truth is, I don't like them at all. To be perfectly honest, I hate them. As far as I'm concerned—and both my grand-fathers held the same view—a dog is a mangy cur, a syco-phant, a howler, a biter, a bootlicker. What is there to like in a dog?

And even if I did have positive feelings for dogs, they would have vanished after that lawsuit.

The door to Father's courtroom opened and a tall, heavy-set man entered. He wore a gray jacket, gray trousers, and a gray hat. His clothes were flour-dusted. Zanvel was his name, and he was a baker on our street. In the courtyard where the bakery was located, he was often seen walking about wearing only his long underwear, a pair of crumpled slippers, and a conical paper cap instead of a hat.

Journeymen bakers earned good money, but Zanvel worked in his father's bakery and was paid better than the others. He had pale skin, blue eyes, and the thick neck and shoulders of a boxer. He kneaded huge chunks of dough, the sort of work that can easily break someone who isn't strong enough.

He approached Father's desk, pounded it with his fist, and said, "Rabbi, I want to start a lawsuit."

"Against whom?"

"My wife."

"Sit down. What is it?"

"Rabbi, it's either me or the dog," Zanvel shouted. "There's no room in the house for both of us."

"Who is this dog?"

"It's not a person but a real dog," Zanvel yelled. "She wanted to have a dog in the house—a fire in her kishkes! Ever since she got that dog, she's forgotten she has a husband. My line of work is hard and backbreaking. I'm a baker, Rabbi. I bake bread so people can eat. All night long I work non-stop in the bakery, but when I come home in the morning, instead of being greeted by my wife, a dog comes bounding toward me. He barks and jumps on me. They say it's out of love, but I don't need his love. It wouldn't be so bad if it were a little puppy. But this dog is like a bear. A wild beast. I don't want a wild beast in my house. He opens his mouth like a lion. He can crunch a hard bone. When he barks, I have to cover my ears. He makes such a fuss, I'm lucky that he doesn't bite my nose off. What do I need that for? My father didn't have a dog.

"People say that a dog is useful if you live in a village, out in the country—but why do I need a dog in Warsaw? No one's going to rob me here—I have an excellent lock on my door. Poor people used to come to my house and I would give them what I could: one or two groschen, a piece of bread, a piece of sugar. But this dog drove all the poor people away. I have a charity box hanging on a wall and a Hasid used to come to collect the money, but he stopped coming, too. If we don't chase the dog away, he'll end up tearing the hem of someone's coat. These Hasidim are scared of dogs."

"Why does she need a dog?" Father said.

"Rabbi, you know like I know. No one in my family owns a dog. She began complaining that she's lonely. You see, we don't have children and she wants to have a living creature in the house. So I tell her, get a cat or a parrot. At least a bird sings. A parrot speaks. But what does a dog do? Rabbi, I'm ashamed to say it, but she kisses him. She's always kissing him. I'm not, like they say, jealous. But when I see her kissing him, it wounds me to the core. Rabbi, I work long, hard hours for her—and it's the dog she kisses. She never stops kissing him, petting him, worrying over his health. He doesn't eat enough; he doesn't sleep enough.

"Rabbi, I told her I'm going to take a piece of iron and split his skull open. So she screams she'll leave the house. Rabbi, I want to have a rabbinic judgment! I want you to decide which of us is more important—a man or a dog."

"What kind of comparison is that, God forbid. Comparing a dog to a man!"

His wife was summoned. A sturdy woman came in; she had a high bosom, strong arms, thick calves. Her shoes were tattered. She didn't walk but dragged the soles of her shoes along the floor. She was sucking on a hard candy and one red cheek was pulsating. Boredom radiated from her face.

"Why do you need a dog?" Father asked her. "The Talmud teaches that a Jew is forbidden to keep a savage dog in his house."

"He's not savage, Rabbi. He's better than this one," she said, pointing a short, stubby finger at her husband.

The argument lasted a long while, and from their wrangling I, a little boy, clearly understood that the woman loved her dog and hated her husband.

Father finally succeeded in reconciling husband and wife. He apparently convinced the woman to either sell the dog or give him away. But hardly a month had passed and the man returned.

"Rabbi, I want a divorce."

"Who are you?"

"I'm the baker who was here once. My wife still has the dog. The rabbi decided then that—"

"Yes, I remember."

"Rabbi, it's the same as before. Even worse. She sleeps in bed with him. If I'm lying, may I drop dead right here."

Father sent for the woman once more and—wonder of wonders—she came with the dog. It was a huge pug, fat and thick-legged. From his wideset eyes and flaring nostrils gleamed a rage, a hatred, a contempt for every living creature. The dog barked at my mother. The woman wanted to take the dog into the courtroom, but Mother declared, "There's a Torah in there."

As soon as I entered the kitchen and saw the dog, a mixture of dread and joy overcame me, somewhat akin to the feeling I had when a policeman came to our apartment. I took a piece of bread and threw it to the dog. As he sniffed, it, the brown eyes in his wrinkled forehead seemed to say, I don't consider dry bread a treat!

I wanted to pet the dog, but his growl frightened me. This was no dog but a four-legged anti-Semite. Each limb breathed fierce aggression. When Father heard the barking in the courtroom, he too became frightened. He closed the holy book he was studying and began fanning himself with his yarmulke.

"What's that?" he said.

"That's her husband," replied Zanvel the baker.

Usually Father attempted to make peace between litigants, but this time he did so merely for appearance's sake. As bizarre as it sounds, the woman agreed to a divorce. She sacrificed her husband for a dog.

I don't remember if the divorce was performed in our house, but the marriage was dissolved. The woman remained in the apartment with the furniture. The street seethed with the news: a dog had driven a man away from his home. The women said awful things about the wife, whispering secrets into one another's ears.

One woman who heard the news turned red, exclaiming, "No!"

"Yes!" the other woman replied, and whispered another secret into her ear.

"Foo! How's that possible?"

"Everything is possible, my dear woman. May she burn in hell!"

"And I once heard a woman tell a story about a noblewoman who lived with a stallion, a male horse, and they had a baby that was half human and half colt."

"What did they do with it?"

"It died right away."

"All of this stems from excessive luxury. Having it too good drives them crazy—a fire in their kishkes!"

After his divorce, Zanvel went downhill. He started drinking. At night, while kneading huge chunks of dough, he'd sing plaintive tunes, and his voice could be heard throughout the courtyard. The neighbors complained that he woke them up. People wanted to arrange a match for him. All kinds of women flattered him, but he didn't want any of them.

"If a dog can drive me out of my house, then I'm really afraid."

And he was seen frequenting the tavern on our street.

The woman with the dog found another man, a fruit dealer, and it was rumored that he would soon marry her. He happened to like dogs. When he visited the divorcée, he brought her chocolates and jellybeans, and a piece of meat or a bone for the dog. If the woman was busy, the fruit merchant would take the dog out for a walk, leading him on a leash. Sometimes he would unleash him and the dog would follow him warily, dragging the leash on the sidewalk.

An awful thing happened on one of these walks. Zanvel the baker was approaching the dog. He was barefoot, wearing only a pair of white long johns and balancing a cheesecake on his head. Zanvel had ceased kneading the huge chunks of dough at his father's bakery because he had developed a hernia. Now he was working for a pastry baker, who had sent him to deliver the cheesecake to a café.

When the dog saw his onetime master and rival, he attacked him with savage fury. The cheesecake fell off Zanvel's head.

The dog bit Zanvel's foot and Zanvel grabbed hold of the dog's neck and strangled him. The fruit merchant pulled out a knife and stabbed Zanvel . . .

All of this took place within a few minutes. The policeman blew his whistle. Someone telephoned the first-aid squad. On the ground lay the dead dog with bloodshot eyes, a smashed cheesecake, and a bloody human being. The dog's tongue was black and hung out of his mouth like a rag.

Soon Zanvel the baker was placed on a stretcher in the first-aid wagon. A medic bandaged his foot and the shoulder the fruit merchant had stabbed. The policeman handcuffed the fruit merchant and brought him to the police station. A janitor took the dead dog away. Barefoot boys and girls and even a few older fellows picked up pieces of the cheesecake and nibbled at them. When the woman, the owner of the dog, heard what had happened, she ran out into the street to bemoan her dog, and perhaps her lover, too. But the women on the street immediately pounced on her, beat her, and pulled fistfuls of hair from her head. There was a wild free-for-all on the street with tempers flaring everywhere.

You probably want to know, dear reader, how the story ended, and I'll oblige. The end was that the fruit merchant, after spending a couple of weeks in jail, disappeared. Zanvel the baker lay in the hospital two days and then returned home. He went to console his former wife—and once again a match ensued. Before the wedding the wife swore that she would never again keep a dog in the house.

Instead of a dog she bought a cage with two yellow canaries and a green parrot to boot. Zanvel the baker resumed working for his father. He no longer kneaded the huge chunks of dough but slid the loaves of bread into and out of the oven. Zanvel's canaries chirped and sang all day long. The parrot spoke Yiddish. Everything was fine and dandy once again. In my view, heaven and earth had sworn that a dog must not be victorious. And as proof we have the story of *"Chad Gadya,"* the last song sung at the Passover Seder, where the dog is on the side of justice but the Master of the Universe is on the side of the stick that beats the dog. Because whether just or unjust, a dog should not interfere with our affairs.

That's the interpretation attributed to the rebbe, Reb Heschel, who supposedly first told it. And even if he did not, he *could* have told it.

NICE JEWS, BUT . . .

ঙাঁ

A couple of times my father judged big lawsuits in his court-room. A "big" lawsuit usually lasted days, and each side had an arbitrator who served as a kind of lawyer. When businessmen and rich Jews came to us, Father sat in front, the arbitrators on the side, and the litigants a little farther away. They yelled, spoke, argued, wrote numbers on sheets of paper, and smoked cigarettes and cigars. Mother brought in glasses of tea with lemon and biscuits.

And I would stand behind Father's chair, listening and watching.

One lawsuit was particularly complicated because it was never clear who was suing whom. The owner of a store had died, leaving heirs. Partners too remained. The heirs and the partners were in total disagreement.

The heirs were all modern young men and women. The men wore Western clothing; either their beards were trimmed or they were smoothly shaven. The women wore hats, not mar-riage wigs. The partners were Hasidic Jews.

Days passed and it was difficult to ascertain what was going on and why the heirs and the partners couldn't come to terms and continue running their business. Gradually the cat came out of the bag: the partners were stealing. The heirs, however, did not want to make this accusation at first. They insinuated, asked naïve questions. They brought in a bookkeeper, who did not speak to the point but stammered. My father was not fit for such conflicts. He didn't know his way around numbers. Furthermore, he trusted people. The thought that somebody could be dishonest never occurred to him. In addition, the partners were Hasidim. They spoke of their rebbe. They sprinkled their conversation with Torah learning. They smoked thick cigars and grandiosely blew smoke rings. They all had apartments, wives, daughters, and bookshelves full of holy texts. So how could one be suspicious of such Jews?

But I, the little boy with the red sidecurls, realized what was going on here. Behind their beautiful words, the heirs were accusing the partners of theft. The partners never clearly denied it but argued, What do you mean? You're suspecting Jews like us? If that's the case, then it's the end of the world! . . . Words like that should not even be brought to one's lips! . . . It's a desecration of God's name.

After a while the matter became clearer. The Hasidic Jews did not steal, God forbid, they just helped themselves. They were giving themselves loans. They took money under all sorts of excuses and chicanery. They had to marry off daughters, send wives to spas, go to spas themselves, and all that cost money. And since the old man who had just died had been a bit senile during the last few years, the young partners had slipped him papers to sign, which he did. They had conspired with the head bookkeeper. They bought merchandise for the store, paid double the cost, then got hefty kickbacks from the wholesalers. True, they didn't break into safes, but nevertheless they did take money that did not belong to them. They did this cleverly, pre-meditatively, on a grand scale, and respectably, as befitted Hasidim who sat at the head table with the rebbe when they traveled to see him for the holidays.

When Father finally grasped what was happening, he seemed to shrink into himself. His face fell and became pale; his beard seemed to become knotty. He apparently lost the ability to speak. Instead, he continually sighed. Behind him stood the Holy Ark. Above it, on the ledge of the Holy Ark, two lions held the tablets with the Ten Commandments. All day long the com-mandment proclaimed: Thou shall not steal!

Mother brought Father tea, but he let it grow cold. He lit a cigarette, but immediately put it aside. The partners attempted to share an aphorism, a Hasidic commentary, a clever remark made by Reb Heschel, but Father paid scant attention to them. His sad eyes asked, What good are all these beautiful remarks if . . . if . . .

Suddenly one of the heirs lost patience and yelled, "You're all thieves! Swindlers! Connivers! Crooks!"

For a while the courtroom was silent. It seemed to me that after these words the world would be torn asunder. But the kerosene lamp continued to burn. Then another heir shouted, "You'll be led away in chains!"

A wave of fear came over me. I actually felt my red hair standing up on my skull. One of the partners, a man with a long black beard, called out, "You can talk with such chutzpah, but I want you to know that you can't do anything to us except sprinkle salt on our tail."

"Thief! Pickpocket!"

"Atheist! Infidel! Lecher!"

It soon became clear that the partners were not only thieves but wily thieves as well. They raked it in in such a fashion that they were perfectly right in the eyes of the law. They had come to the rabbinic judgment because they wanted to continue on in the store. Their arbitrator argued, "We want peace, but if you want war, there's going to be war."

"Give back what you've stolen!"

"Atheist! Sinner of Israel!"

"It is absolutely beneath our dignity to continue talking with them," declared one of the partners, a man with a wide yellow beard and gold-rimmed glasses.

Father gazed at him in astonishment. His blue eyes seemed to ask, Since you're a thief, why is talking to them beneath your dignity? Instead, he said, "I don't have Cossacks or policemen here—I can render a decision only according to the Torah."

"We know the law . . ."

Father beckoned the partners' arbitrator to speak to him privately.

The man said, "We have to tell them to come to terms."

"Are the partners ready to return the money?" Father asked.

"Nothing returns from the cemetery," the arbitrator answered cleverly.

"Then how can they come to terms?"

"We have to find some kind of ruse . . ."

"What kind of ruse?"

"Here's the situation. If the partnership is dissolved, both sides will be denied a livelihood. One needs the other. So we have to find a device to pacify them."

"What kind of device?"

"We want the wolf to remain whole and the sheep to remain whole . . ."

"How can Jews do something like that?"

"Oh, Rabbi, you're so naïve."

Later, Father called the heirs' arbitrator for a private talk. "What can be done here?"

"What can one do? Every one of them is a veteran thief. Each one of these partners can put the best pickpockets to shame. They have swindled so much that years will pass and we still won't be able to come to an understanding . . ."

"Didn't they make a living?"

"They made plenty."

"Then why did they do it?"

"They just did."

"Well, well, it's time for the Messiah to come," Father declared. "Ah woe, it's time . . . it's high time!"

"They did it so cleverly that the only ones who'll be jailed are the bookkeeper and the cashier," the arbitrator said. "But what will the upshot of all this be? Just like each one of them goes to see the rebbe, so each one of them can steal with his eyes closed."

"How do we know they won't keep doing the same thing?" Father asked.

"There's no guarantee . . ."

The lawsuit dragged on and on. Now they yelled, and now they spoke amicably. The man with the black beard described the beautiful wedding he had given for his youngest daughter. The Viennese hall was full. The young couple got a pile of wedding presents. Two klezmer orchestras provided music. The rebbe himself officiated at the ceremony.

Then Father exclaimed, "It must have cost you a fortune!"

"Maybe we put aside so much every week."

Father looked at me and seemed to ask, Does it pay to be a swindler for this?

No, these people did not steal or swindle because they needed money for bread. They stole in order to travel to the spas and stroll along on the promenades, to give huge dowries to their daughters and buy jewelry for their wives, to stay in fancy hotels and travel second class on the trains.

Late at night, when all were gone, I asked Father, "How can pious Jews behave like this?"

"Little silly, if they behave like this, they are not pious."

"But they take trips to see their rebbe."

"So they go."

"But everyone thinks of them as pious."

"Never mind what everyone thinks. The Master of the Universe cannot be fooled."

"Perhaps God, too, can be fooled?"

"Rascal!"

The next morning when the heirs and the partners returned, Father told them, "You've sat here for days and your idle chatter has prevented me from studying the holy texts—but I cannot render a decision. You don't have to pay me. I don't want to be involved in this case any longer!"

"Then why did you start?"

"I thought it was just a simple dispute . . . but since the matter is as it stands, how can you come to terms? The first thing to be done is—as the Torah states—return that which is stolen. If one steals, one must return the theft—even if it's a penny."

"But, Rabbi, I didn't realize how naïve you are!" the partners' arbitrator called out.

"I don't want to take the responsibility for such things . . . If you want to come to terms, come to terms on your own."

The partner with the black beard glared at Father, seeming to stab him with his black eyes. The partner with the yellow beard made a face as though he had tasted something sour.

The other arbitrator suggested that Father have a private talk with him, but Father said: "I'm not discussing this matter anymore."

Everyone departed, leaving behind smoke and little saucers full of ashes and cigarette butts. Mother came in to clean up. Her face was aflame.

"So what did you gain by doing this?" she asked.

"I couldn't continue. The entire matter is thoroughly disgusting," Father replied.

"How will the children eat?"

"If there's nothing to eat, they'll fast," Father answered, annoyed.

The litigation upset Father. He said to me, "Don't think that all Jews are like this, God forbid. For every thief there are lots of honest people. But one doesn't hear about them. These people are out-and-out hypocrites. The Talmud states that seven years after a hypocrite's death he becomes a bat."

"Are these Hasidim going to become bats?"

"If the Talmud says so, that's what they'll become."

"When?"

"Don't be in such a rush. The Master of the Universe has time."

I imagined how the partners would become bats. The first one to become a bat would be the partner with the black beard; then the partner with the yellow beard would become a bat. They would fly about at night and girls would be frightened lest the bats fly into their hair . . . I began to lose my respect for these people who speak beautifully, smoke expensive cigars, make expensive weddings for their daughters, and travel to spas. Secretly, they are thieves. They will end up as bats.

THE GIFT

ℒᴑᴂ

My thoughts return to my father's courtroom and I remember a lawsuit which I should have written about long ago.

The door opened and a woman came in who looked both Hasidic and secular. She wore a long coat and high-heeled shoes. She was in her thirties, with a pale face, blue eyes, and regular features. Her curled marriage wig was artfully combed into her own hair. She looked like someone who lived in what we called the "other streets"—she was not from our poor street. A respectable tidiness encompassed her. My father didn't see her, but he already knew it was a woman by her footsteps, and so he turned aside so as not to look at her.

"What can I do for you?"

The woman did not reply at once. Her mouth moved like someone who wants to speak but is choking on the words. Finally, she uttered, "I need some advice . . . I mean, I want to institute a lawsuit."

"Against whom?"

The woman seemed to swallow something. "My husband."

"Where is he?"

"At home."

Father began asking her questions. The woman's responses were so muddled that Father sent me to call the husband, who lived on Khlodna Street. The woman gave me money for a droshky. It was one of the few times that I rode all by myself in a droshky without packages. But it was a shame that Khlodna Street was so close—the ride was over before I had a chance to enjoy it.

I rang the bell to a well-to-do apartment. The door was opened by a short man with a pointy little beard wearing a Western-style suit but no tie. He looked at me in astonishment. I knew that I shouldn't break the news to him all at once but, rather, prepare him in a sensitive manner. But I didn't know how, so I said, "Your wife is calling you to a rabbinic judgment."

The man looked askance at me.

"Who are you?"

I started telling him everything. He heard me out and screwed up his face as though he'd tasted something sour. A shudder ran through him. He took hold of his pointy little beard and for a while stood there stunned, indecisive, embarrassed. Then he declared, "Well, it's too late."

"Your wife is in a hurry. She wants you to take a droshky."

"What? Oh, all right."

The man went to another room and returned wearing a tie and a derby. In his hand he held a narrow walking stick. Outside, he took a droshky, but he didn't say one word to me during the entire trip. He sat shrunken into himself, looking like someone who had suffered a terrible humiliation, a wrong that could never be made right. A sort of sadness came over me, too. What could this woman possibly want from him? I asked myself. It seemed that the young man was angry at me for being the messenger, and again I could not enjoy the droshky ride.

I brought the defendant to our apartment and stood in a corner waiting to see what would unfold.

"What's the problem the two of you have?" Father asked.

"I don't know anything about it," the man said with a wave of his hand, as if to say that he knew nothing of either the problem or the solution.

"Who is suing whom?"

"Clearly, she's suing me."

"What's your complaint?" Father asked the woman, and turned his face away from her even more.

Again the woman began choking on her words—she looked as if she had swallowed something. "Rabbi, I want a divorce."

"Tell me why."

"Rabbi, you can't call what we have a life. In good families a man pays attention to his wife. But *he* doesn't pay attention to me."

"What do you mean by 'attention'?"

"For a woman support is not enough. A woman wants to have a good time once in a while, to get some pleasure out of life. In good families couples go places—to the theater, to the movies, to a dance. They come, they go, they invite people to their house. They visit others. A woman wants to be seen. But with him I sit like a bird in a cage. All day long he's in the store. And as soon as he comes home, he starts working on his account books. Our store is closed on Saturday and Sunday, but we don't go anywhere Saturday or Sunday either. And that's how the years fly by, and life becomes boring. Sometimes I feel so suffocated I just want to put an end to my miserable life . . ."

Now the woman could no longer suppress her anguish. She burst into a hoarse cry, just like one of the common women of our street. While the woman spoke, the husband stood and gazed at her, stunned and confused. He looked as if he couldn't believe his ears. Occasionally he cast a glance at the door as if prepared to flee without replying.

"Do you have children?" Father asked.

"No children, none," the woman replied. "But I don't even want to talk about that. That's God's will, even though all my sisters have children and I'm the only one chastised that way. The doctor told me it's his fault. I am able to have children!"

And the woman burst into tears again.

Father rubbed his forehead. "So, then, what is it you want?"

"Rabbi, this is no life. I pace back and forth in my apartment as if in a prison cell. There's a story about a bird who was put into a gilded cage—and that's me. One day is like another. Holy Rabbi, I'll give you an example: In good families men occasionally give their wives a present. You would think it's foolishness—after all, I can buy myself whatever I wish. But it's nice when a man brings something home. It's not so much the present but the fact that the man thinks of you. My brothers-in-law always bring my sisters presents. We have a telephone and they call me and say, 'Guess what I got today.' They got this, that, and the other thing. Even if it's a trifle, for a woman it's important. But with us years go by and I don't get even a penny's worth of gifts. I'm ashamed to say it, but since we got married I've never gotten a thing from him—so rather than live such a life . . . I'd rather . . ."

Now the woman began crying even more bitterly. She pulled out a little handkerchief and blew her nose. Her weeping made her body tense up and twitch. It seemed to me that this tension would cause all her clothes to split at the seams, her corset would pop open, and she'd stand there stark naked. It dawned on me that my father, too, never brought home any presents. I didn't even know that a husband is supposed to give his wife gifts. Presents were given to a bride or a groom, not to one's wife.

I looked at the man; he stood there open-mouthed. His face expressed anguish, astonishment, and something else that could not be named. Despite his anxious state, there still was a touch of laughter within him, which I couldn't understand. Father covered his eyes with his hand. He rocked back and forth as if unsure of himself. He apparently didn't grasp what the woman wanted and why she was crying so bitterly.

"And what do you say?" he finally asked.

"Do you mean me, Rabbi?" the man said.

"Yes."

"Rabbi, I'm going to tell you something interesting."

"All right."

"Rabbi, it's true that we don't go the theater or to the movies, but it's not because I'm stingy. I provide her with the best and finest of everything. The money drawer isn't locked; it's wide open for her. She can buy herself whatever she pleases. But what does one get out of the theater? A couple of fools dress up like Purim players and that costs you several rubles. In the movies you see absolutely nothing. Just something that looks like a fiery rain and small people running around moving their lips as if mute. I always tell her, if you want to go to the movies, go with your sisters."

"I want to go with you, not with my sisters," the woman groaned.

"I don't like it. It's sheer torture for me. If I have time, I prefer picking up a newspaper and reading an article that deals with practical matters, current events, politics, and so on. What good is the theater? You come home late, and then you can't get up in the morning. And I don't go dancing either. I'm not a dancer, and standing there watching others dance is not my idea of fun. If she wants to go dancing, she can go. Her brothers-in-law run to these dances and they'd take her along. I don't dance and I don't leap. I like to sit in my chair and read the newspaper and do my accounts. So what are we left with? Only her complaint about presents. And now, Rabbi, I'd like to tell you something that will amaze you."

"What is it?"

"It so happens that just today I bought her a gift. Well, actually, I bought it a week ago, but the jeweler delivered it today. It's true that I'm not a big gift giver, because I hate those cheap trinkets which you buy today and four weeks later are already broken or rusty. I've wanted to buy her a present for the longest time but didn't know what to get. Recently, I had a talk with her about jewelry and discovered what she liked. In short, I went to a jeweler, a fellow from my hometown whom I trust, and ordered a brooch from him for three hundred rubles. Do you hear, Rabbi, for three hundred rubles?

Today I come home from lunch and am surprised to see that my wife isn't there. I fix myself something to eat and am about to return to my store when this little boy suddenly comes in and tells me my wife is summoning me to the rabbi. Precisely today, when I bought her the brooch for three hundred rubles, which is actually worth four hundred—" The man broke off.

Just then I understood the slight amusement in his glance. The woman fell silent. She raised her eyes, stared, gaped. An unearthly silence reigned in the room.

"Well, in that case, everything is fine now," Father said.

"If only she had waited one day," the man murmured.

"Rabbi, there comes a time when one's patience bursts!"

And the woman broke into tears again. It was the weeping of a broken heart, the weeping of someone who has lost everything.

Then Father said, "Well, since he has bought you such a gift, it's a sign that he's devoted to you . . ."

"Now he's really going to lace into me," the woman said, choking on her words.

"Go home. Go home. Let there be peace. It is on peace that the world is founded," Father said.

"Well, I'm going," the man said.

"How much do I owe you, Rabbi?" the woman asked.

"Nothing."

"Then I'll give the boy something," the woman said, looking at me.

"Don't give him anything. He buys candies and ruins his teeth," Father said.

Now tears came to my eyes, too. With these words Father robbed me of a great treasure and many pleasures. The woman surely would have given me a big coin. As I ran to the kitchen to cry, the man and his wife left, walking apart from each other with heads bowed and bearing the burden of humiliation that can never be expunged.

FREIDELE

෨෬

The following happened in our apartment:

The man's name was Yechiel and his wife's Freidele. They had a shop on our street and I knew them both. He was tall, thin, swarthy, with a long neck, a pointy Adam's apple, a high forehead, and a long nose. Even his beard was long and narrow. Were the store his alone, no one would have come to shop there, because he was grumpy and absentminded. People spoke to him, but he didn't hear.

If a customer told him, "Reb Yechiel, give me a pound of sugar," he would bring a pound of flour.

"What are you doing? I wanted sugar!"

"All right, sugar it is. Just a minute."

And he would return to the customer with a bag of salt.

He would have had to close up his shop long ago, but Freidele was the exact opposite of her husband. She was short, roly-poly, red-cheeked, with an endearing smile. She listened to everyone's orders, rushed to give the customer what he wanted, and had a nice word for everyone. She was able to attend to several tasks at once: count money, chat, weigh merchandise. If someone bought on credit, she didn't write the sum in an account book. She remembered everything. Freidele would often tell her husband that he wasn't needed in the store and that he was no help at all. Furthermore, Yechiel would drive customers away. He would wander about the store, move here and there, biting the tip of his beard as if deeply pondering the philosophy of commerce. Although he did nothing, his gaberdine was dusted with flour and stained with oil. Freidele would call him over to the counter. "What are you thinking about? Why the cat has whiskers?"

"Leave me alone," Yechiel would grumble in reply.

Suddenly Yechiel fell ill. His situation soon became critical and the doctors didn't know what was wrong with him. Some people assumed that the angry and sad thoughts that had passed through Yechiel's head all these years had fused into a poisonous knot. On Monday he lay down in his bed, and by Thursday he was a transformed man, yellow as wax, gaunt like after a long fast. His lips were white and his huge eyes terror-stricken. Freidele spared no money. She organized a concilium of doctors and professors, but each offered a different diagnosis. It was clear that Yechiel's time had come. Freidele's crying mingled laughter and tears. She paced back and forth in the rooms wringing her hands.

"He's a goner," she cried out. "A goner!"

Before he died, Yechiel called Freidele to the bed and groaned hoarsely, "Give me your hand!"

Freidele gave him her hand. Hers was warm; his was tepid and damp.

"Promise me that you won't marry anyone else," he moaned. Freidele's red cheeks turned white. "Well, as you wish," she promised.

Soon thereafter Yechiel sank into a coma from which he never recovered. How strange it was that this grumbler, whom everyone in the street hated, had a big funeral. At the cemetery Freidele wept her mingled laughter and tears and then returned home to sit shiva. I forgot to mention they had no children.

At the conclusion of the shiva, Freidele reopened the store. Now that Yechiel no longer wandered about in it, there were even more customers than ever before. The store was always full. Freidele served with incredible speed and reckoned all the charges in her head. Business was so good she had to hire an assistant, and later another girl as well. She had to enlarge her store, because it was always crowded and there was no room to move. Matchmakers inundated her shop, offering marriage partners, but Freidele gave them all the same reply.

"I can't marry. I gave him my promise."

Learned Jews explained to Freidele that a promise like hers need not be kept. Such was the decision rendered by a series of rabbis in similar circumstances. But Freidele replied that she had no intention of breaking her oath.

"I've lived my life," she said. "I'm done with playing and dancing."

From her sly smile it was hard to tell whether she was sad or indifferent. She was the sort of woman who was called impassive and phlegmatic—nothing bothered her.

Freidele was a conundrum. She talked little about herself. No one knew what was going on inside her. Was she sad? Happy?

At times, it seemed Freidele was so immersed in business there remained no time or energy for any other thoughts. She lived out her life entirely among sacks of flour, sugar, and dried beans.

One day the door to our apartment opened and Freidele entered. She wanted to speak to Father. A while later he called in Mother. This is what had happened:

Freidele had become acquainted with a salami merchant, a widower her age, and she wanted to consult Father on a religious matter: Would she be allowed to break her promise? If yes, she would like Father to officiate at a quiet wedding. Freidele did not want to delay matters. She paced about in Father's study, occasionally glancing out the window at her store, which happened to be exactly opposite us. It was hard to imagine that this businesswoman could love anyone. The entire match was probably a calculated move. According to Freidele, a husband and wife couldn't manage two stores. The widower had a big shop. Freidele was apparently ready to put on a white apron and cut salami, chicken breast, liver, and cold cuts with a long knife.

Father consulted one book after another. Then he asked Freidele if she had given her oath of her own free will or out of fear lest she upset her ill husband and thereby aggravate his condition. From the way Father formulated the question he practically put the answer into her mouth.

"What could I have done?" Freidele said. "He was on his deathbed."

"That means you did it for his sake."

"Of course!"

Father hesitated a long while. It wasn't easy to take responsibility for such a matter. Nevertheless, he ruled that the widow was permitted to marry. I thought that Freidele would be over-joyed, but she wasn't the sort of woman who displayed her feel-ings. She immediately began to discuss practical matters. She wanted to know the cost of the wedding ceremony and declared that there be no guests. Father suggested that they have a minyan. Plain folk from the street could be brought in, or even some young boys. Freidele evidently intended to sell her store or give it to someone else. She wanted to keep everything secret. Was it perhaps because she was ashamed before people?

Mother expected Freidele to pour out her heart to her, as did all the other women, and even some men as well. But Freidele said, "I left the store unattended. I must run back right away."

As soon as she left, Father resumed studying. Mother walked about absorbed in thought.

"Freidele is a strong person," she said.

And although I was a little boy, I understood what she meant. It was unusual for a woman to have such a resolute char-acter.

A few days passed. At our house everything was set for the wedding: the bottle of wine, the blank marriage contract ready to be filled out, and the canopy with the four wooden poles which stood in its usual place next to the stove. What else was needed? No one on the street knew what was about to take place.

Early one morning someone knocked on our door. There stood Freidele. I scarcely recognized her. Her formerly red-cheeked, round face was now long and pale. Her eyes looked confused and frightened. She wore a shawl over her head like a poor Jewish woman. I think her shoelaces were untied. Even her voice had changed.

"Is your father up yet?" she asked me.

"Yes."

"May I come in?"

"Of course."

Freidele went into the rabbinic courtroom. I wanted to follow her, but she said sternly, "I have a private matter to discuss with your father."

I remained in the kitchen, but I was transformed into one huge ear. Freidele spoke softly in the other room and Father answered her. Then Freidele spoke again and I heard soft sobbing. Shivers ran down my spine. Not only had I never heard Freidele crying, I couldn't even imagine her shedding tears. Even at Yechiel's funeral no one had heard Freidele weep. In the bedroom Mother, too, had evidently overheard Freidele's sobs. She put on her robe and slippers and came into the courtroom. For a long time one could hear whispers, sobs, interrupted exchanges, and suppressed sighs coming from the room.

No matter how hard I tried to hear what was happening, I could make out nothing. It dawned on me that perhaps Freidele's fiancé had died. But why would they have to whisper so much about that? I tried to open the door, but Mother immediately yelled, "Shut the door!"

Only later did I learn what had happened. At night, after Freidele had fallen asleep, Yechiel had come to her, dressed in his shroud. He shouted fiercely at her and tried to strangle her. In the courtroom Freidele had shown Mother a blue mark on her throat. Her arms and breasts were full of black-and-blue marks, which were called "dead man's pinches." It was obvious that there, in the other world, Yechiel didn't want his wife to marry. He shouted into her ears, beat her, warned her that she would marry under a black wedding canopy and die a premature death.

Father no longer wanted to take the responsibility upon himself. He told Freidele to go see a rebbe. Such matters were not within a rabbi's purview but could be dealt with better by a Hasidic rebbe.

To this day I don't know if Freidele went to consult a rebbe or what he may have told her. But nothing came of the match with the salami dealer. Freidele remained a widow for as long as we lived on our street. At home I was told not to say a word, God forbid, and I learned early on to keep a secret.

For a couple of years Freidele was like her old self. Her cheeks glowed. Her smile was both friendly and contrived. She measured, weighed, talked with her customers, bossed around the girls in her employ. No one could have guessed that she had undergone an awful, terror-laden experience. Then suddenly she began to age. As if overnight the skin on her face became wrinkled and crow's-feet developed around her eyes. She stopped smiling like a woman and now had the smile of a grandmother. Her voice softened. Her head began shaking as if always nodding yes.

The story of Freidele's dream terrified me. I often thought of Yechiel and his appearing to Freidele clad in his shroud, which frightened me, too. What would I do if he came to me in a dream? And how would it have harmed Yechiel in the next world if Freidele had married the salami dealer?

People on the street did not know what had happened, but they spoke of her often. What had she gained by doing such

FREIDELE

good business and amassing so much money? What good did her fortune do her? She opened her store very early and closed it later than all the other shopkeepers. On Sabbaths, Freidele ate on the balcony of her apartment and watched the world pass by below.

When I returned to Warsaw after a trip to see my grandfather, I no longer saw Freidele in her store. She was probably where Yechiel was. But did she become his footstool in heaven, as Jewish folklore declares? It's no good being the footstool for such an irascible person. But on the other hand, from a psychological point of view, Freidele's dream was a reflection of her own desires. Subconsciously—at least that would be the Freudian interpretation—she probably had loved her husband very much.

REB ZANVELE

On a bench near the stove in the Hasidic *shtibl* sat several Hasidim. Around them stood some young men and boys, listening to Reb Zanvele the *toomtoom*.* Reb Zanvele was tall, broad, with the big head of a scholar, a high forehead, deep wrinkles in the corners of his eyes, and sidecurls down to his shoulders.

But, alas, he did not have a beard. His face was as smooth as a woman's—even worse than a woman's. It did not have even a trace of hair. His beardless face bore testimony that Reb Zanvele had earned his nickname. His voice was a little deeper than a woman's, but not as deep as a man's. He said, "He who was not present at the Alexander Rebbe's court on the second night of the holiday has no idea what pleasures this world can offer. And of the world to come, it goes without saying! Oh my, what do today's Hasidim know about Hasidism? He who has not known the rebbe cannot know what a wise man is! His wisdom cast a glow over the world. He could do everything at once: study Talmud with commentaries, chat with young people, and hear what a boy was saying at the far end of the study hall. He came

*_Toomtoom_, a Talmudic word signifying a nonvirile man.

140

up with witty sayings that made you explode with laughter, but when you recalled them later, you realized that they were also profound and deep, deep as the ocean."

The Hasidic rebbe whom Reb Zanvele praised was in a way similar to Reb Zanvele. That rebbe was a eunuch, which is also a kind of *toomtoom*. In praising the rebbe, Reb Zanvele was also subtly lauding himself. The Hasidim understood this and exchanged glances as they listened. Yes, one can be either a eunuch or a *toomtoom* and also have a great soul. One thing has nothing to do with the other. Even the prophet Isaiah consoled the eunuchs who kept the Sabbath and did good deeds. Nevertheless, it was still a humiliation to walk about with a naked face among an entire congregation of bearded Jews. Indeed, although Reb Zanvele was not married, he wore a tallis when he prayed. He had no source of income; the Hasidim sup ported him. Reb Zanvele either studied or prayed or paced back and forth in the *shtibl* deep in thought. He smoked a long pipe, and from a little ivory box he sniffed snuff into which he had mixed a couple of drops of brandy in order to make it stronger. Occasionally he would approach a young boy, pinch his cheek, and ask, "So what's going to be, huh?"

He lived in a little rented room somewhere. On Sabbaths he was invited for meals, but going to a stranger's house was painful for Reb Zanvele. Women and girls were somehow afraid of him, and terribly embarrassed, too. Since he wasn't a man, then in a way he belonged to their gender.

Once, a girl began laughing at the Sabbath table and couldn't stop. Reb Zanvele knew quite well she was laughing at him. But what can one do? If it was ordained in heaven to be a *toomtoom*, and a pauper to boot, one must bear the yoke. While the girl was laughing, Reb Zanvele perused a Pentateuch which happened to be on the table. As he read the commentaries, he took hold of his beardless chin and began tugging at it as though a beard were growing there.

"What a delight! Sweet as sugar!" he said.

On another summer afternoon, while Father sat in his courtroom writing his commentary and Mother read a book in the kitchen, the door opened and in walked Reb Zanvele the *toomtoom*. Following him was a woman. She wore a wide-brimmed, satin-fringed bonnet decorated with little glass beads, a satin coat, a beaded dress, and pointy shoes that looked as though they had been made in the Middle Ages. On her beaked nose sat a pair of brass-rimmed glasses. One look told us she was a rebbetzin.

Reb Zanvele hurried in to see Father, for it wasn't his habit to speak to women. After Mother welcomed the woman, she remained for a while in the kitchen.

"Rebbetzin, I am the Chentchinner Rebbetzin. My late husband was the Chentchinner Rebbe."

"Oh! Please sit down."

"I can stand. Rebbetzin, do you perform weddings here?"

"Yes, why not? Small weddings with just a wedding canopy."

"What else do I need? A tumultuous wedding? I would like to get married to Reb Zanvele."

Mother stood there tongue-tied. She seemed embarrassed. Seeing me, she called out, "Why are you hanging around in the kitchen? Go into the other room!"

I was dying to hear the rebbetzin explain why she was marrying the *toomtoom*. But I also wanted to hear what the *toom-*

toom himself would say about this. I went into the bigger room and heard Reb Zanvele speaking.

"Her husband was a great scholar. One of the very great ones. He left sixty books."

"Sixty? Published?"

"Well, here's the story: They're all in manuscript. His handwriting was very hard to decipher. She wants me to get his books published."

"Where are you going to get the money?"

"She wants me to sell advance subscriptions."

"That's going to be very hard."

"Jews are generous. I've never done this sort of thing before, but I'm getting older and I can't wander about anymore. Eating at strangers' tables is painful for me. This way I'll have another human being in the house."

"It's not unreasonable."

"So since she's willing, what can *I* lose?" Reb Zanvele asked.

"You're absolutely right."

"I would like you to officiate at the ceremony," said Reb Zanvele.

I looked at Father. I wanted to see in his eyes a trace of amazement, some of the bewilderment I had detected on Mother's face. But Father wasn't surprised at all.

"Well, fine . . ."

"Uh, do we need some refreshments?" Reb Zanvele asked.

"Well, you will need wine for the blessings. But the custom is to offer the minyan some cake and brandy."

"Fine, we'll have it. I see you're studying the Tractate *Bekhoros*," Reb Zanvele said, changing his tone.

"I'm writing a commentary on Rabbi Yom-tov Algazi's*
book, *The Laws of Yom-tov,*" Father declared.

"Oh, really? Well, everything is useful. In a couple of hundred years somebody will write a commentary on *your*
commentary."

I saw at once that the conversation was not heading in the
direction I wanted it to go and I quietly returned to the kitchen,
where I could hear the woman.

"Yes, we spent fifty years together, but one cannot remain
alone. I come home on Sabbath from the synagogue and I have
to go to a neighbor's house to hear the Kiddush. My neighbor is
a tailor, but he pronounces Hebrew like a boor. Reb Zanvele,
alas, is not healthy, but he is a learned man. What more do I
need at my age? I am not the matriarch Sarah who gave birth
when she was ninety."

"Yes, I understand."

"He promises me that he'll get my husband's manuscripts
published."

"Well, perhaps . . ."

"My late husband, may a bright Paradise be his, wasn't well
either. Unfortunately, he was sickly all his life. I was as healthy as
a giant and I've remained that way. May no evil eye harm me, I'm
already sixty-eight years old and I still have all my teeth. But
don't judge me by the way I look now. I once was a beauty . . ."

"One can see it on you."

"I used to dazzle the entire street. They wanted to match me
up with a merchant's son, a strapping young fellow, but my good

*Yom-tov Algazi (1727–1802), a famous rabbi, was the author of *The Laws of
Yom-tov,* a commentary on *Bekhoros.* (Author)

mama—may she intercede on my behalf—wanted to have a son-in-law with a rabbinic ordination. Nowadays they ask the girl what she wants. In my day children weren't asked their opinion. Right after the wedding he started ailing and remained ill for the rest of his life. He lay in bed and studied. For days on end. All night, too. So since I was deprived throughout all my young years, what do I need now? I'm afraid of just one thing: I hope he doesn't hold it against me."

"You mean your husband?"

"Yes. After all, a hundred years from now I'll be in Paradise with him."

"Everything will be as it is destined to be," Mother replied.

Despite the fact that we did our best to keep the wedding a secret, people on the street and in the courtyard learned about it. On the evening of the wedding, youngsters tried to break into the apartment. Father went out to meet them.

"So you've come to mock, eh? What is there to mock here? Reb Zanvele is a scholar."

"But he's missing something!" one of the youths yelled.

"Everything he has is a gift of God," Father responded. "Go home. The world is not under the rule of chaos!"

But the street youths and the low-class girls who had gathered at our steps apparently thought that the world was indeed ruled by chaos. When the groom passed by the steps, they greeted him with catcalls and katzenjammer music. One of the youths hooted, "*Toom* . . ." and another concluded, "*toom!*" Girls laughed lasciviously.

A shoemaker came running and yelled at the youths: "With one slice of a knife we can make you just like *him* . . . You ought to be ashamed of yourselves!"

Making fun of a person with a defect has vexed me terribly ever since I was a little boy. I thought it grossly insensitive and indescribably cruel. But most boys my age could not comprehend this. They would run after a hunchback. They would shout nasty nicknames at every cripple. They would chase a madman and pull all kinds of terrible tricks on him. Woe, I myself was not totally innocent of this sin. I would make fun of fools. But isn't a fool also a human being with a defect? Can a fool make himself wise? And why does an ox deserve to be slaughtered? Can an ox transform itself into a human being?

The shouts and catcalls directed at Zanvele the *toomtoom* continued throughout Father's entire reading of the marriage contract and the wedding ceremony, too. Even the men who had been called in to complete the minyan made jokes and winked at each other. The woman, the rebbetzin, nodded her bonnet-bedecked head. Reb Zanvele wore the white *kittel* grooms wear to remind them of the day of death. By the light of the kerosene lamp his beardless face was white as chalk. In fact, he looked very much like a priest. His eyes shone with both chagrin and laughter. It seemed as if his eyes were asking, Is this what human beings are?

The quorum of Jews departed after the ceremony, but Reb Zanvele and his new wife sat in Father's courtroom for a long while, because they didn't want to pass through the crowd that awaited them. In the meantime, Reb Zanvele told stories about Hasidic rebbes. I no longer remember about which rebbe he spoke, but he said, "Standing by the mezuzah, he prayed that large numbers of people would not come to him."

"Really?"

"Relatively few people came. Even on Rosh Hashanah the study house was half empty."

"He didn't take any money either, did he?"

"God forbid!"

"Every Hasidic rebbe has his own way," Father stated. "The Rizhiner Rebbe used to ride on a coach with silver wheels . . . The Rimanover Rebbe used to sniff snuff from a golden box."

"Don't you think I know that? But why does a rebbe need a golden snuff box?"

"The Holy Temple was also made of gold."

"And so was the golden calf, forgive the comparison."

Soon the street youths and the low-class girls tired of waiting. They dispersed and silence reigned. Reb Zanvele and the former rebbetzin bade us good night. The rebbetzin had her own apartment and Reb Zanvele went to sleep there.

I lay in bed until late at night unable to fall asleep. By then I already knew some of the secrets pertaining to the sexes. I recalled the shoemaker's words: "With one slice of a knife we can make you just like him."

What kind of strength was it that could be sliced away with a knife? A knife could make a thousand men *toomtooms* and eunuchs. One pin could blind a thousand seeing eyes. One stone could break a million people's heads. So how then can a human being consider himself so high and mighty? I liked the rebbe who took no money better than the rebbe who rode in a coach with silver wheels.

That night I wanted to become a rebbe to whom only a select few would come. And I wouldn't take money from them. God forbid! And I would sniff snuff from an old little wooden box, just like the one my father had.

THE BRIDE

When our kitchen door opened and a man dressed in a long gaberdine entered, it by no means meant that the visit would elicit any income. Such a man might have come to ask a question about ritual, or for some advice, or just to chat with Father. Quite often, respectable men would come requesting a contribution for a bride's dowry, a Visit the Sick fund, or to sell Father an advance subscription for some scholar's religious commentary. There were many reasons why a Jew would come to see the rabbi.

But the situation was entirely different when a young man dressed in modern clothes visited. Someone in Western dress did not come to ask for favors or contributions. A young man like that came in to either break an engagement, get a divorce, or for a like matter which brought in a few rubles.

The modern young man who came in one time looked particularly engaging. He wore a derby, a stiff collar, a striped tie, and held a walking stick in one hand. He wore spats over his low-laced boots. A little mustache grew above his upper lip. His jacket was unbuttoned and from his vest dangled a watch chain.

He brought into the house an aroma of chocolate and perfumed soap. He came in smiling and gave a little bow.

"Is the rabbi at home?"

"Yes, please go into the next room."

Father stood next to a prayer stand over a sacred text, writing a commentary on a sheet of paper. He was composing a treatise in defense of Rashi, covering the entire Talmud, where he refutes Rabbenu Tam's assertions that there are contradictions in Rashi's commentary.

"Good morning."

"And a good year! What can I do for you?"

"Can we arrange a wedding here?"

"Of course."

Father asked the young man to be seated. In such cases Father immediately asked if the bride and groom had parents. But it turned out that both were orphans on both sides.

Father sighed. "Well, everything is fated."

From poor people Father asked three rubles to perform a wedding, but this time he requested five. The young man immediately took out a crisp five-ruble bill and paid in advance. Then he took out a silver cigarette case and offered Father an aromatic cigarette. He did everything quickly and gently.

Father bore a grudge against the modern secular types, the dandies, the heretics, but I saw that he was favorably disposed toward this young man, who didn't talk much and who wasn't a pest. Having said what he had to say, he stood up and stretched out his hand to shake my father's. Among pious Jews it was not customary to shake hands prior to departing, but my father was aware of secular customs. At the doorway the young man once again bowed his head to my mother. Then he did something totally unexpected: he gave me a six-kopeck copper coin. I blushed and did not know whether to take it or not. He patted my shoulder and whispered, "Buy yourself some jellybeans."

The young man left behind an aura of affection. The wedding was to take place in a couple of days, and Mother was already curious to see what the bride of such a fine young man looked like. My parents discussed this at home.

Imagine, then, our astonishment when the young man came with his bride and several other young folk, his good friends, and we saw that she had only one leg. Everyone was astounded, except, of course, my father, who never looked at women.

The bride was not only lame, she wasn't much to look at either. She was wide-set, stooped over, not young, and stood on her one foot holding a crutch. The young man introduced his bride to my mother, who, confused and embarrassed, wished her mazel tov. Then everyone went into the other room. One young man had brought a bottle of brandy and a cake in a paper bag. These types of weddings were over quickly. Father had already prepared a printed marriage contract and had only to enter the names of the bride and groom. I ran down to the Hasidic *shtibl* and called in a couple of men to complete the minyan.

The wedding canopy with the four poles was always placed next to our oven. The white robe that the groom wore, the *kittel,* lay in a drawer. Father did everything demanded by Jewish law and tradition. According to custom, the bride has to circle the groom seven times, following the Biblical verse in Jeremiah: "A woman shall go around a man." For the limping bride this was not an easy task. The banging of her crutch on the floor echoed dully throughout the apartment. Even a blind man would have been able to see that the bride was lame, but my pious father neither saw nor heard. He recited the blessings; the groom declared the bride to be his wife; then Father recited the concluding blessings and congratulated the couple.

After the ceremony the gathered guests celebrated at the table with sponge cake and brandy.

After everyone had gone, Mother entered the study. "Well, what do you say?"

"What should I say?"

"Why would such a young man marry a cripple, poor thing?"

Father shrugged. "A cripple?"

Then Mother said to Father what she usually did under such circumstances: "Oh, are you naïve!"

Then she described the bride. Father did not consider it so bizarre. "So what's the big deal, marrying a cripple? Doesn't the hymn 'A Woman of Valor' state: 'False is charm and beauty is vanity'? What difference does it make if the bride has two feet or one? The body is only a body."

But Mother rebuked him: "If you didn't see her then at least you should have heard her banging with her crutch."

But with a wave of his hand Father made naught of the entire situation. First of all, he hadn't heard any banging. Second, how could he tell what was banging? "Oh, what nonsense!" Father said, returning to his study of the Talmud and other holy texts. Rabbenu Tam, the great scholar and grandson of Rashi, had posed a very difficult question—one as strong as a stone wall—about a Rashi commentary, and Father had to show that the holy Rashi was correct.

Mother returned to the kitchen. She walked about agitated. Mother liked to grasp things logically. Puzzles annoyed her. What did such a good-looking young man see in such an ugly woman? How could such a match have been made? A woman neighbor came in and claimed it all stemmed from love. People who fall in love are blinded, dazzled; they lose their head. Then she began to tell all kinds of stories about love affairs—how girls were passionately in love with men who were blind, mute, hunchbacked, and who-knows-what. The truth of the matter was that my mother knew of more examples than did the neighbor, but all these incidents still could not answer her question.

"Perhaps she has lots of money," the neighbor declared.

"How much money could she have? To spend your entire life with such a cripple! . . . Something is wrong here."

I too was astounded. I listened to all the neighbor's clever explanations, but I paid scant attention to them. After a while she left and Mother said to me, "How come you're spending all your days in the kitchen? Better pick up a holy book and study."

And she chased me into Father's study. I opened up the bookcase and began rummaging among the books. I looked for one with blank inside covers, and with a pencil began drawing all kinds of little men, animals, flowers, and grotesques. I was still a small boy then, so I was permitted to look at women. I had already had my fill of seeing all kinds of mystifying things in this room, and my head was full of ideas and fantasies. It struck me that perhaps the bride and groom were not people but demons. And perhaps the bride had once been a princess who was now disguised as a lame woman. Perhaps the young man was a wizard from Madagascar who had cast a spell on her. In the storybooks I had read I had come across many such tales. Even then I felt that the world was full of great mysteries.

I don't know how much time passed, perhaps four or five days, perhaps a week, when suddenly I heard a heavy banging on the staircase. I pricked up my ears. Mother listened attentively, too. Someone was knocking on the door. I opened and saw the lame bride. God Almighty! She had become years older. She was bent over, seemingly broken, and her face was red and swollen. I backed away and she limped in, thumping dully with her crutch.

"What happened?" Mother asked.

"Rebbetzin, he's killed me! Slaughtered me without a knife! . . . Woe unto me and woe unto my life! That thief, that murderer, that killer, that wretch!"

"Sit down here. What happened?"

"He cheated me out of everything, that ganef, that crook, that louse! . . . Rebbetzin, it would've been better if he had killed me. What should I do now? Where can I go and who can I turn to? Dear rebbetzin, that was no man but an Angel of Death!"

The door was open and neighbors came streaming in. The lame woman was sobbing bitterly, pinching her swollen face, wringing her hands. Her words tore at your heart. She was an orphan, she said, had no mother or father. All her life she had been working as a maid in other people's homes. He had sidled up to her with smooth talk and sweet words. He loved her, he said. He would carry her in his hands. She would be the crown of his head forever. How could she have known that he was just sweet-talking and bluffing? She believed him, woe unto her senses. She gave him everything she had, down to her last penny.

For a couple of days after the wedding he was as good as an angel to her. She was happy, in seventh heaven. Then suddenly he fled, that murderer, that hangman, that skunk, that apostate! He stole everything from her. Even her wedding band. Even the presents that he himself had given her, even her wedding clothes. He left her absolutely naked . . . Oh, Mother! He'd gone to America, crossed the sea, gone off to the far edges of the world! And now she was a deserted wife, a bleak and hapless *agunah*! Wouldn't it be better if she were a corpse lying with her feet toward the door and shards on her eyes?

The woman yelled, wailed, cursed, and the neighbors cursed along with her. They heaped upon that charlatan all the maledictions, plagues, ulcers, blisters, and afflictions that Warsaw Yiddish possessed. Mother stood there white as a sheet with an expression of utter sorrow in her blue eyes. One puzzle had been solved, but an entire pack of new ones had overtaken her: How could this young woman have believed him? And above all, how could a young man who seemed to be so fine and sensitive have such a murderous heart? Didn't he know that she was an orphan? Didn't he see she was, alas, a broken cripple? How lowdown and mean could a person be? What thoughts ran through that wicked man's head as he sailed across the ocean at night? How could he sleep after having committed such a grievous wrong? How can one sully one's soul in such a manner? Ah, woe, how great is the evil impulse!

Later, Mother came into the courtroom and told Father the entire story. He turned pale and for a long while could not say a word. Finally, he remarked, "Well, what can one expect? That's what happens when one does not believe in the Creator!"

He turned and looked at the Holy Ark, which was always covered with a curtain. There were two open-mouthed little lions with small tongues at the ledges and between them the two tablets of the law with the Ten Commandments. All day long these tablets proclaimed: I am the Lord your God . . . Thou shalt not murder, Thou shalt not steal, Thou shalt not commit adultery, Thou shalt not covet . . .

Whosoever does not hearken to this voice lives in a lawless world, a world of absolute chaos.

HAD HE BEEN A KOHEN

ൟൟ

The door opened and a bareheaded woman came in. It was rare for a woman to enter our apartment with her head uncovered; even those women who went about bareheaded would don a kerchief before coming in. But this woman was apparently too upset, too agitated to think about anything else besides her shame and utter disgrace. She was of average height, rather chubby, with a florid face and blondish hair combed back in a bun and held together with hairpins. This woman had surely once been a beauty, but now she looked disheveled, bitter, and angry. She had already begun yelling in the kitchen.

"He's a murderer! A bandit! I can't take it any longer! I want a divorce! A divorce!"

Evidently, Mother knew her. She lived across the street from us at 15 Krochmalna Street. Amid shouts and curses, she described what her husband, that outcast, that scoundrel, was doing. He wasn't supporting the family, he paid no attention to the children, he spent days on end in the tavern at 17 Krochmalna drinking with hooligans and loose women. But the trick he had pulled the other day went beyond all bounds. This she wouldn't keep quiet. This she wouldn't forget even when she lay with her feet toward the door and shards on her eyes.

"What did he do?"

"Rebbetzin, he gambled away our stove!"

"The stove? How can one gamble away one's stove?"

This man apparently didn't have a built-in tile stove in his apartment like we did; he had a removable iron stove. And it was this stove that he had lost at cards. Men had come into the apartment and removed it.

The woman was shrieking away in an unearthly voice. Mother usually attempted to make peace among couples, but this incident touched her to the quick. Embarrassed at how low a man could sink, she stood there silent. The woman began enumerating an entire list of flaws, one worse than the other. Mother was so preoccupied with the woman she didn't even notice me there. Under different circumstances she would surely have chased me away. I had already known that people commit all kinds of wrongs, but I had never heard of such abominations. Who could have imagined that such evildoers were living so close to us?

Father sent me to summon her husband, and I went with great curiosity. I climbed up to a high story and found a half-opened door. Several children were playing, yelling, screeching. On a broken sofa lay a man, fat, unshaven, with a thick yellow mustache, wearing a shirt with a studded collar and boots with matching high bootlegs, the sort that were worn by hooligans and common riffraff. He was bareheaded and his sandy-colored hair was closely cropped. He looked sleepy, drunk, and angry.

"What do you want?"

"Your wife is summoning you to the rabbi."

"To the rabbi, eh?"

"Yes."

"Does she want a divorce?"

"Yes."

"Fine. I won't keep her!"

The man stood up. He told the older girl to keep an eye on the little children. A couple of minutes later he was in Father's courtroom. His wife greeted him with curses, shouts, and balled fists.

But he let out a roar and drowned her out: "Be quiet! If you want a divorce, there'll be a divorce! Just stop shrieking!"

Father called Mother aside for a private chat. Mother maintained that the quarreling couple should not be divorced because they had children. Father agreed. When he returned to the room where the couple was waiting, he told them what he usually did in such cases: A divorce is no small matter; such things should not be done rashly. One should give it serious thought; one must consider the children.

The woman started fuming. "In that case, I'm going to go to another rabbi."

"No other rabbi will give you a divorce on the spur of the moment."

Father smiled slightly as he said this. He had lied in order to keep the peace. There were indeed rabbis in Warsaw who didn't stand on ceremony and performed quick divorces for whoever wished one. One rabbi in our street, whom I will not name, especially excelled in these instant divorces. Who knows, perhaps he was driven by need. That rabbi actually had a divorce factory—

on occasion there were several scribes sitting in his apartment simultaneously writing bills of divorce. Warsaw rabbis had often spoken of proclaiming his divorces invalid.

For a long while husband and wife sat in our apartment insulting and cursing each other. The racket could be heard in the street. The woman recounted all her husband's nasty deeds and all the trouble and humiliation she had suffered at his hand from the day her horrible luck had driven her to marry him. At one point she cried, at another she yelled at the top of her voice; now she spoke softly, as though pleading, and then once again she became wild. Her hands were always groping for something. Had she found an object in our apartment with which to hit her husband or throw at his head, she certainly would have done something wild in her murderous rage. But there was nothing for her to grab except books. The man hardly said a word. When he did open his mouth, he spoke like a boor who was both afraid of and prepared for battle.

After lengthy arguments and complaints the couple departed. Warsaw was a huge metropolis and even Krochmalna Street was a big city. Several days passed, perhaps even a few weeks, and we heard no news about the couple. A quarreling couple was no big deal! It happened every day, even ten times a day. Indeed, there were couples on Krochmalna Street who would go out to the street when they wanted to fight and wait for a crowd to gather. What sense was there fighting in one's own apartment in front of the four walls?

Suddenly one day the door opened and the man who had gambled away the stove at cards entered. He seemed thinner, rumpled, neglected. His cheeks were hollow, his formerly ruddy face now pale. His mustache wasn't twirled upward like a spring but drooped miserably like that of a down-and-out janitor. Even his boots had lost their former shine.

"Is the rabbi here?"

"Yes, in the next room."

For a while the man was silent. Mother was silent, too, but I sensed that both of them wanted to talk. Finally, Mother asked what had happened.

"Oh, Rebbetzin, things are bad."

"What? Tell me."

"They divorced us."

"Where?"

The man mentioned the street.

Mother clapped her hands in dismay. "Shame on them! For a couple of rubles they're ready to destroy people!"

Silence fell once again. Then Mother asked, "What are you? A Kohen? A Levite? An Israelite?"

"Me? Um, I don't know."

"Did your father ever give the priestly blessing in the synagogue?"

"My father? Give the priestly blessing? No. Why do you ask?"

"Go in to see my husband."

Mother, a rabbi's daughter, knew very well what she was asking. A Levite or an Israelite is permitted to remarry the woman he has divorced. But a Kohen is forbidden to marry a divorcée, even if it is his own ex-wife.

The man was filled with regrets and he poured his bitter heart out to my father. He had been angry, his wife had been in a foul temper, too, and a rabbi had coveted those couple of rubles. And so he divorced them, one two three. But their anger passed. The children were crying and longing for their father. His wife was beside herself. He, too, longed for his wife and kids something awful. Yes, he knew that he had behaved badly, but he wanted to become a decent person once more. He had vowed never to touch cards again. He would stop drinking. He loved his wife and he was a devoted father. He was ready to give up his life for his children. And he wanted to remarry his loyal wife.

"You are not a Kohen?" Father asked quickly.

The man said no, but Father sent me to get the man's ex-wife and tell her to bring either the divorce document or her marriage certificate. Father confirmed that the man was not a Kohen. He was happy. Mother's mood improved as well. Now that the harm could be rectified, Father began preaching to the man: Aren't you ashamed of yourself? How can one be so deeply involved in sensuality? Man's soul stems from the Throne of Glory. It is sent down into this world to be improved, not spoiled. One does not live forever. There comes a time when a person must give an accounting . . .

The man nodded in agreement to everything that Father said. The woman stood there wringing her hands—not in the courtroom, but in the kitchen doorway. In the interim she had also become pale and melancholic. She showed Mother that she had lost so much weight her dress was falling off her shoulders. She could not sleep at night. There was a knot in her throat and she couldn't even cry . . .

Suddenly she began wailing in a voice so fearsome it was hard to imagine it could be human. I understood then that husband and wife loved each other with an enormous love and were bound to each other with a force that no divorce could rend asunder.

Yes, that rabbi, the manager of that divorce mill, had taken those couple of rubles. But the wedding took place in our apartment. Bride and groom laughed and wept under the wedding canopy. The next Sabbath, husband and wife were strolling arm in arm on Krochmalna Street, accompanied by their little children. A terror comes over me when I think what would have happened, God forbid, had that man been a Kohen . . .

ONE GROOM AND

TWO BRIDES

ℒℴ

The door opened and two men and two women entered. I knew
three of them. One was a scribe who lived in our courtyard, a
man reputed to be a saint. It was said of him that every time he
wrote God's name he went to the ritual bath. Writing a mezuzah
or a couple of passages for a set of tefillin took him days or
weeks. He was, alas, dirt-poor. Poverty was visible on his pale
and wrinkled face; his yellow forehead was lined like parch-
ment. His beard was dirty gray and sparse; his sidecurls hung
down disheveled. A profound piety glowed in his eyes. This man
was a tzaddik, a righteous, saintly man who never forgot his
Creator for one moment. He lived in perpetual need, obeyed the
commandments, and did good deeds. Father stood up the instant
he saw him, just as one rises before a great rabbi. Father would
often say that this scribe always had the name of God before his
eyes. He seemed to have stepped out of an ancient time.

The scribe was a widower. His daughter, an old maid of forty,
accompanied him. She was short, fleshy, with a milky face and
two large, calflike eyes. She was cross-eyed, and half-blind to

boot. She managed the scribe's household. Ah, woe unto such household management! They lived in a garret. The scribe was always observing fast days and his gaberdine was full of patches. His finest garment was his set of ritual fringes.

I knew the other woman as well. She was tall, thin, dark as a shovel. She worked at the baker's at 12 Krochmalna Street and often stood outside holding a basket of rolls. She was forty as well and was considered a fool, a simpleton.

The second man was about sixty, with a round, grayish beard. He had on a small cap, the sort worn by common folk, and a short jacket spotted and stained with glue. I didn't know him. He looked like someone who glued sacks.

After Father had offered a chair to the scribe, he asked him how he was, and the scribe replied, "God be praised." When he uttered these words, he began shaking and quaking. It was no trifle, mentioning the Creator of the Universe, the One who had created heaven and earth! The man seemed enveloped in holy texts.

"What can I do for you?"

It turned out that all four had come for a Din Torah, a rabbinic judgment, and that the plaintiff was none other than the scribe. Here is the story:

The poor scribe had longed to bring his daughter under the wedding canopy, and this sixty-year-old man, a divorcé, had come along. The scribe had an engagement contract drawn up, promised the man a couple of rubles dowry, and the match was concluded. But what was the upshot? It turned out that the man also had another fiancée; indeed, it was the swarthy old maid who worked for the baker. The scribe did not want to humiliate the other man, God forbid, his daughter's fiancé. He accused and defended him simultaneously. The gist of his remarks was that this man had made a mistake and had been tempted to transgress. But errors must be corrected, and so the scribe was demanding that the other fiancée step aside and that his daughter, God forbid, not be humiliated and made into a laughingstock. One could see that the scribe was terribly upset. He stammered and was in constant fear lest he say words one was forbidden to utter, and lest, God forbid, he unwittingly shame the other man. The scribe's awe of God hung over him like a sword, for every bad word can bring down upon a person the fire of hell and the nether depths.

After the scribe had finished speaking, the swarthy old maid found her tongue. "Rabbi," she said in a hoarse voice, "I don't know this man and I don't know his daughter. This man here wanted to marry me and he gave his word. He told me nothing about this other one. I've slaved away enough at the baker's. I too want to come to an agreement. I'm not a young girl and I've knocked around bakeries and kitchens long enough. I'm a human being, too! I should drop dead right here if I knew anything about her. I swear to God I don't know her from Adam. And what does he need a wife like that for? She's not for him. He needs somebody who can help him in his line of work. What can she do? Just look at her, Rabbi. She's blind."

Father banged the table, signaling her not to speak in such a vulgar manner. But she continued spewing fire and brimstone. She called the scribe's daughter a slattern, a hunk of dough, a blind cow, a filthy slob, a fool, and other such names.

The scribe's daughter began to weep. The scribe bent his head, murmuring through his bluish-white lips. He was probably whispering that he forgave this woman the humiliations she was causing him and prayed that she also be forgiven in heaven. Father pulled out his pocket handkerchief and wiped his moist eyes. Yes, such was the destiny of the righteous: they have to suffer here on earth.

Then Father addressed the other man. "You became engaged to the daughter of a scholar. Your future father-in-law is a tzaddik. His daughter is a respectable young woman, and God willing she will be devoted to you. So what made you think of bothering to turn someone else's head? What are you? A youngster? Do you think the world is lawless? There is a God in heaven who sees everything! A person does not live forever! Someday you'll have to give an account of yourself . . ."

Father was angry. He threatened the man with all the measures of hell. He even told him he would have to apologize to his future father-in-law and recalled the saying in the Ethics of the Fathers: "The bite of scholars is like the bite of a fox, their sting is like the sting of a scorpion, and all their words are like fiery coals."

Hearing Father's praise, the scribe shrunk into himself. He began to sway back and forth and shake his head from side to side—he was not a scholar and he was being undeservedly praised. The scribe was afraid that all those words might cause him to forfeit his share in the world to come.

The common Jew tried to justify himself. He said that he had had no dealings with the swarthy woman. She had approached him, not he her. He had come to buy rolls from her for breakfast and she had started chatting with him. This led to that, and they went to a café for some cheesecake and coffee.

Well, after some more of this and that, she talked him into marrying her. He told her that he was already engaged, but she didn't want to hear about it. After more this and that, he made his promise. What should he do? If the rabbi says that he has to send her away, he will send her away. After all, one cannot have two brides at once.

"What do you mean, you're going to send me away?" the swarthy old maid yelled. "What am I, some kind of rotten apple that can be thrown around? You didn't tell me about another fiancée. If I had known that you had a fiancée, I'd have left you and sent you to the blazes so quickly all your bones would've broken. You thief, you liar, you sweet-talker, you heretic! And this cost me money, too, Rabbi . . ."

The woman began to reckon up all the expenses she had had and the other men who had wanted her. Because of this heretic, this old roué, she had lost many precious bridegrooms.

My father heard her out. He shut his eyes and rested a fist on the kerchief which was used to signify agreement among the litigants. For years he had been the rabbi on this street, but he still could not get used to these people. I felt I could see his thoughts behind his forehead and in the little veins in his temples, and how he was trying to stand up for these ignoramuses who, poor things, wanted to be Jews but did not know how. After a while he seemed to wake up. The contenders had run out of arguments. He let each of them touch the kerchief. Finally, he rendered his opinion: the swarthy bakery woman must step aside, because the man had already been engaged to the scribe's daughter. But since she had had expenses and perhaps felt humiliated as well, she would have to be paid two rubles in compensation for stepping aside. I remember feeling ashamed after hearing this decision. Two rubles was so insignificant a sum even for such paupers. I felt myself turning red, but I saw at once that, as usual, my father had had a better grasp of the situation than I.

The swarthy old maid tried to bargain, saying that the sum was too small, but I saw that she was amenable. The fiancé with the gray beard immediately stated that he had no money. Where would he get two rubles from? He had to marry and rent an apartment, and he didn't have two rubles to throw around. Then the scribe raised his head and mumbled that since he wanted his daughter's situation resolved, he would pay the two rubles.

And with a shaking hand he began to dig into his pockets and take out groschens, kopecks, coins of various denominations. He counted, made errors, didn't recognize the coins, swayed, and never stopped praying. And that's how he counted out those two rubles. The swarthy woman gathered up the coins and left in a huff, cursing and slamming the door, as if to say she was still dissatisfied and could not be bought off with two rubles.

This Din Torah in and of itself was bizarre, but a couple of days later we heard someone fiddling with our door handle. Mother went to open the door and the scribe came in. With tears in his eyes, he told Father that the man who planned to marry his daughter was not even divorced. Father was incensed. He summoned the man and called him a scoundrel, a sinner, a heretic, and other names that rarely passed my father's lips. The man listened with a guilty look on his face and responded, "I'm in the process of getting a divorce."

"You troublemaker! You said you already were divorced!" said the scribe.

ONE GROOM AND TWO BRIDES

"I didn't say that."

"You *did* say it," the scribe bore witness. "Would I have arranged a match with a married man?"

The fiancé tried to deny it, but my father drove him away. It seems to me that he even cursed him. The scribe remained in Father's study. Father wanted to repay the two rubles, but under no circumstances would the scribe accept them. Both men sat there for a long time discussing holy texts and sighing at the state of the modern world.

"Ah, woe and alas, it's the end of the world. It's high time for the Messiah to come!" Father exclaimed.

"Well," the scribe sighed. It seemed as if he was mutely saying, We can't offer our suggestions to the Master of the Universe.

After a while the scribe passed away. His daughter remained a spinster. She became totally blind and sat on a doorstep collecting alms. For a long time thereafter I used to buy rolls from the swarthy old maid. She, too, never married.

When some years later I became a bar mitzvah, my father gave me a set of tefillin made by that holy scribe, and I always seemed to feel on my forehead the sanctity that exuded from the Torah verses he had written.

AN UNUSUAL WEDDING

Krochmalna Street was packed with houses of ill repute. In Yiddish they were called "little houses," but the streetwalkers lived in cellars whose windows looked out from under the entrance steps. The men who patronized those places had to crawl through dark, cave-like corridors. At the square, thieves and pimps hung out. Even in those years I knew that there were prostitutes and that it was forbidden to look at them, because a single glance could make one impure. But I didn't give much thought to precisely what they were or what they did.

I often saw them standing by the gate or at the square, their cheeks rouged and their eyelashes mascaraed, wearing flowered scarves and red or blue shoes. Occasionally, one of them smoked a cigarette.

When I passed by, they would call me names: "Hey, you little jerk! Hey, you sneaky little Hasid! Hey, you dummy!"

But now and then, when one of them gave me a little piece of chocolate, I would run off and throw it into the sewer. I knew that whatever they touched was defiled. Once in a while they would come into our house to ask questions pertaining to religion. Mother would be embarrassed, unable to utter a word. But it made no difference to my father. He turned his glance aside from all women in any case. Their questions always pertained to the *yortzeit,* the anniversary of a loved one's death, the only *mitzvah* the streetwalkers observed. They could never figure out the precise day on the Jewish calendar to light the memorial candle.

Once, a young man came in who looked like an artisan. He wore a little Jewish cap but a short jacket and buttoned shoes. His shirt had no collar, just a paper dickey from which a tin collar stud stuck out. He was unshaven and his cheeks were hollow. His aquiline nose was pale as though from an illness. His big black eyes shone with a mildness that reminded me of fasting and funerals. This is how mourners looked who came in to ask questions about sitting shiva and observing the thirty days of mourning.

Mother happened to be in the courtroom, and I sat over a Talmud and pretended to study.

"What can I do for you?" Father asked.

The youth began to stammer and turned red, then pale. "Rabbi, is it permissible to marry a prostitute?"

Mother was shocked. Father asked the young man a question and looked at me sternly.

"Leave the room!"

I went to the kitchen, and the young man remained in the courtroom for a long while. Afterward Mother came into the kitchen and said, "There are all kinds of lunatics in this world!"

Father decided that he could marry the prostitute. Not only was it permissible, but indeed it was a *mitzvah* to rescue a Jewish girl from sin. The young man needed no more. He immediately requested that Father officiate at the wedding. He left in high spirits and gaily slammed the door. Father came into the kitchen.

"What kind of madness is this?" Mother asked.

"He has—how do they say it over there?—fallen in love."

"With a prostitute?"

"Well . . ."

Then Father returned to his holy text.

I don't recall how much time passed before the wedding took place. The girl had to count the prescribed number of days after her menstrual cycle and then go to the ritual bath. All kinds of women helpers began swirling around her. Everyone on the street knew what was happening and they discussed it in the grocery, the butcher shop, even the synagogue. Usually, only a few people attended a small wedding. My father would almost always have to send me to the Hasidic *shtibl* to gather enough men for a minyan. But this time our apartment turned into a Viennese salon. Every minute our door opened and in walked a thief or a pimp. But most of the guests were promiscuous girls fancied up in silk and velvet, and wearing hats with ostrich feathers. The madams came, too.

The fact that an honest young man had fallen in love with a whore was a victory for the underworld, especially the women. They saw it as a sign that there was hope for them, the rejected ones, too. The madams donned their marriage wigs and shawls, which they wore to the synagogue on Rosh Hashanah and Yom Kippur. The streetwalkers wore long-sleeved dresses without corsets. They kissed the mezuzah upon entering and politely greeted my mother. Mother stood there pale and disheveled. Our neighbors encircled her like a guard so that, God forbid, none of the impurity would rub off on her. But no change was visible on my father, who wasn't bothered by any of this. He stood by his prayer stand studying a text and even wrote some comments on a sheet of paper. Everyone was waiting for the bride and groom.

From the balcony I could see people waiting on the sidewalk and by the gate. Several girls and madams joined me on the balcony. Suddenly there was a commotion. The couple had emerged from some courtyard, accompanied by an entire entourage. The bridegroom was spruced up in a new summer jacket and lacquered shoes. The bride, small and swarthy, looked like a girl from a fine middle-class family. The women on the balcony pulled out little hankies and began wiping away their tears.

"Look how pale she is!"

"Is she fasting?"

"She's pretty as a picture!"

"I wish it'd happen to me!"

"God willing, may it happen to you!"

"Here they come! Here they come!"

"One should never lose hope!"

A huge pimp, blind in one eye and with a jagged scar on his forehead, kept order. A madam wearing a wide marriage wig shouted angrily at the girls and told them to stand near the wall. A girl with a face as pockmarked as a grater laughed with one eye and cried with the other. This wasn't just a wedding but a show worthy of Kaminsky's Yiddish Theater. Usually we didn't need a sexton, but the pimps brought one of their own, a short man who mingled with the crowd. When the bride entered the apartment, all the women threw kisses at her. They grabbed her, they hugged her, they didn't want to let her go. They showered her with good wishes. To each one she said the same thing: "God willing, may it happen to you." Each time she said this, all the girls choked back a sob.

Father sat down to write the marriage contract, but then came a tense moment. He began whispering to the sexton. He consulted a holy text. It was senseless to write that the bride was a virgin, but neither was she a divorcée or a widow. Exactly what was done and whether they wrote into the document that the bride was to receive one hundred gulden or two hundred I do not remember.

Four pimps held the staves of the wedding canopy. Since both bride and groom were orphans, they were led to the wedding canopy by the brothel owners and the madams. Everything was done according to Jewish law and tradition. The bridegroom wore a white linen robe, as was the custom. The bride's face was covered by a veil. Father recited the blessings and let the bride and groom sip some wine. When the groom put the ring on the bride's outstretched index finger, saying, "Behold thou art consecrated unto me . . . ," all the prostitutes burst into tears. Even as a child I was amazed by how quickly women start laughing and crying.

After the ceremony everyone kissed and exchanged good wishes. The table was covered with wines, cognac, liquors, all kinds of drinks. Slices of sponge cake were offered as well. The women gingerly picked up pieces of cake with two fingers, pinkies out, taking small bites and little sips like high-class ladies. Today was their day. Today they weren't just whores who lived miserable lives in cellars but friends who had been invited to a wedding. The pimps drank brandy out of tea glasses and began stammering as men do when they become tipsy.

One pimp ran over to Father and yelled, "Rabbi, you are a precious Jew!"

"It's enough just to be a Jew," Father replied.

"Rabbi, I'll take whatever punishments are destined for you!"

"Oh, God forbid . . . one must not talk that way."

"Rabbi, I'm not worth the mud on the soles of your shoes."

Father began looking into his holy books. He wanted these people to leave so he could resume studying. But they were in no rush. They drank and drank. One of the brothelkeepers kept insisting that Father have a drink, too.

"I'm not allowed to drink," Father said. "I have a stomach virus, may it not happen to you."

"Rabbi, it's only forty proof, not ninety proof."

"I can't. The doctor forbade it."

"What do they know? Doctors don't know a thing!"

After a lot of talk, Father finally tasted one solitary drop. The women wanted to take Mother into their circle, but she had already left the apartment. Mother had no intention of mingling with that crowd. I got wine, whiskey, and so much cake and cookies that I stuffed my pockets with them.

The apartment eventually began to empty. I went out onto the balcony and watched the bride and groom being escorted in parade-like fashion back to the courtyard from which they had been led out earlier.

Only when everyone had left did Mother return. It wasn't warm outside, but she opened all the windows to air out the rooms. She threw the leftover cakes and drinks into the garbage. For days afterward Mother went about agitated.

"I'd like to see the day when I can tell this street goodbye," she said.

I heard people discussing this couple for a long, long time. Wonderful things were said about them. A former prostitute was leading the life of a decent wife. She went to the ritual bath every month. She bought glatt kosher meat at the butcher's. She went to the synagogue every Sabbath and holiday. Then I heard that she was pregnant, and then that she had given birth. The women neighbors said that she never even looked at other men. From time to time I saw her husband. The glitter of the wedding day had left him, and he went about once more without a collar, wearing only a paper dickey. Once in a store I heard a woman ask, "But how can a man live with her when he knows where she has bounced around?"

"Repentance helps for everything!" a woman wearing a bonnet replied.

"Still, it's disgusting . . ."

"Perhaps he loves her," another woman called out.

"What's there to love? She's as thin as a stick."

"Every man has his likes."

"May God not punish me for my words!" the woman shopkeeper said. "Mouth, be quiet!" And she slapped her lips with two fingers.

From that time on I paid more attention to the girls who stood at the gates and by the lampposts. Some looked vulgar, fleshy, mean; their heavily mascaraed eyes snickered with a depraved impudence. Others seemed to be so quiet, sad, and shrunken. One of the prostitutes spoke Yiddish with a Lithuanian pronunciation, which was an absolute novelty for us. She came into Esther's candy store and said, "What have you got that's delicious? How about a piece of cheesecake! I've got a hole in my stomach a yard long!"

I heard housemaids in the courtyard saying that the pimps rode around at night in coaches grabbing innocent girls, orphans, and girls from the provinces. They were forced into prostitution and then put aboard ships bound for Buenos Aires. There they had flings with black people. Then a worm would enter their blood and pieces of flesh would fall from their bodies.

These stories were sweet and appalling at the same time. Things were happening in this world. There were secrets not only in heaven above but also down here on earth. I had a burning desire to grow up all the more quickly so I could learn all these heavenly and earthly secrets, to which little boys had no access . . .

REB LAYZER GRAVITZER

ﭪﻭﭪ

Our income limped along, so from time to time my father gave private Talmud lessons to one youngster or another to help pay the rent. One such boy was Dovidl. He had no father and his mother had remarried somewhere in greater Poland. Dovidl was raised by his grandfather Reb Layzer Gravitzer, and he brought a measure of the secular world into our house.

Dovidl was eighteen years old, a handsome youth with black curly hair cut in the "German" fashion. He wore a rather short gaberdine with a slit in the back that reached only to his knees, a collar, a tie, a dickey, and polished chamois shoes. Except for his gaberdine, which looked like a frock coat, Dovidl wore Western-style clothes. His cloth cap was so small it lay on his hair like a tiny pot lid. He wore pince-nez glasses, which hung on a little gilt chain, and of course he had a watch and chain in his vest. He also studied music at the Warsaw Conservatory. It seemed that he wore this slit gaberdine and the small Jewish cap only when he came to study with Father, for Father would not have given Talmud lessons to anyone in modern dress.

This Dovidl was highly accomplished. He was fluent in Russian, Polish, German, and even French, but he spoke Yiddish best of all. He was a fountain of bon mots and witticisms that he had heard from merchants, traveling salesmen, and business agents. He had no great love of learning, but his grandfather had asked Father to give him Talmud lessons several times a week. Dovidl often brought his violin along and would entertain the entire family with the Saturday night "Hamavdil," a Wallachian dance tune, or other traditional melodies. Jokes streamed from him as though he kept them up his sleeve. He could even excel at Talmud when he put his mind to it, which he seldom did.

Even stranger than Dovidl was his grandfather Reb Layzer Gravitzer. Wondrous things were said about him: He looked like a rich man and conducted himself like a millionaire—but reportedly he had more debts than hair on his head. He declared bankruptcy every year, sometimes twice a year. Reb Layzer Gravitzer was a large man with a big paunch, a straight neck, and a leonine head. His white beard was sparse, as was fashionable among wealthy Jews. He wore a hat with a high crown, a collar without a tie, and a somewhat shortened gaberdine. His face was always ruddy. From under his bushy brows gazed a pair of dark eyes, cold as steel.

Everything Reb Layzer Gravitzer did was grandiose. When he blew his thick nose, it resounded throughout the entire apartment. When he spoke, his voice thundered. Each time Reb Layzer Gravitzer came to visit us there was a tumult in the street. He'd arrive in a droshky with rubber wheels. Instead of paying the coachman the usual forty groschen, he'd pay fifty. Poor people besieged him from all sides and he'd hand out four- and six-groschen coins. Even before he knocked, the door was opened for him. The doorway seemed too narrow and low for such a big man. He discussed Torah with Father and wanted very badly to catch him in an error. The truth of the matter was that Father was almost always right. Reb Layzer Gravitzer had already forgotten a lot. But my father was not overly proud and he'd say, good-naturedly, "Well, we'll have a look at the text."

How did Reb Layzer Gravitzer make a living? How could he run such a big house filled with sons, daughters, sons-in-law, daughters-in-law, grandchildren, and maids? What enabled him to travel a couple of times a year to his rebbe, offer generous gifts, bring expensive wine, and pay for the upkeep and lodgings of poor students? In Warsaw, it was estimated that he spent several hundred rubles a week. Where did the money come from?

He had lots of businesses, but Reb Layzer Gravitzer lived on bankruptcies and shady transactions that could have landed him in jail. It was also rumored that he either dealt in or made counterfeit brand labels. People whispered that Reb Layzer Gravitzer bought packets of tea, removed the customs tax stamps by machine, and then mixed the tea with one of inferior quality. He was also supposedly a partner in an illegal lottery. But even though all Warsaw and Lodz knew that Reb Layzer Gravitzer was a bankrupt, a swindler, a schemer the like of which Poland had never seen, he nevertheless always had partners and credit. It was said that he could persuade a stone to give milk. If not for his huge expenses and investments in all kinds of risky enterprises he would have been a millionaire.

Reb Layzer Gravitzer loved two things: prestige and danger. Some people had actually witnessed him lighting his cigar with a five-ruble note. If there was a chance Reb Layzer Gravitzer might get his skull cracked open over a deal and be imprisoned to boot, he'd throw himself headlong into it. He had countless enemies. The rich men of Warsaw and Lodz had often tried to drive him from the marketplace, to get him out of the way, and indeed throw him in jail. Could there have been a greater punishment for Reb Layzer Gravitzer than being forced to wear a prison uniform, wooden clogs, and a round cap, and live among thieves and murderers? Reb Layzer Gravitzer knew that imprisonment was lurking over him. Troops of enemies encircled him. Investigating judges and prosecutors had sworn that they would ruin him. But Reb Layzer Gravitzer knew the law; in fact, he knew the entire legal code. He slipped out of every net and trial. He instructed his lawyers how to argue and what to do. Had Reb Layzer Gravitzer studied jurisprudence at a university, he surely would have been a legal genius. But he used his knowledge only for his own purposes.

Aside from saving his skin through legal trickery, Reb Layzer Gravitzer had also mastered the art of fleeing. Often, when the police came to arrest him, he would escape through a back door, or even out a window and down a ladder. When things got extremely dangerous, Reb Layzer Gravitzer would hide somewhere and lie low for a while. He had hiding places no one knew of, not even his own family. Folks said that illegal merchandise and all kinds of contraband were bricked into every wall of his house. It is superfluous to say that he gave bribes and weekly payoffs to people on the street from the local cop all the way up to the district police commander and even higher. On holidays he sent them wine, cognac, brandy, and money. The word was that there were only two high authorities in Warsaw that Reb Layzer

Gravitzer could not buy off: the minister of police and the governor general. He had tried, but with no success.

It was hard to find two people who were more diametrically opposite than Reb Layzer Gravitzer and my father. But Layzer Gravitzer had chosen my father to teach his grandson. Of course, he ended owing my father money. To whom did he not owe money?

Once Reb Layzer Gravitzer mentioned to my father that he had a sacred text that Father could not find anywhere in Warsaw. Father asked to borrow the book and Reb Layzer Gravitzer agreed to lend it to him. And that is how it happened that I was sent to Reb Layzer Gravitzer's house. Before I went, Mother put a clean shirt on me and combed out my sidecurls. She told me to behave properly and not talk nonsense. Reb Layzer Gravitzer could have sent the book with his grandson, but apparently he wanted someone from our family to see how lavishly he lived.

I no longer recall where he resided, but I do remember walking through an imposing main entrance and climbing up a marble staircase. On each of the enormous doors, decorated with carvings and cornices, was affixed a brass plate with an engraved name. Doctors and dentists lived here. From behind one door I heard someone playing a piano. I rang the bell, but a long time passed before the door was opened a crack and someone peeked at me over a chain. After casting a sharp and searching glance at me, a man asked who I was and what I wanted. Then he told me to wait.

That wait was the longest I had ever experienced. First, I waited for the door to be opened, and then I waited in the corridor. The corridor was full of doors, each one with frosted glass. Telephones rang. Behind those doors women spoke, laughed, sang, and whispered. Then came a leonine roar and I recognized Reb Layzer Gravitzer's voice. Someone led me from one room to another to show me, I suspect, how spacious the apartment was. Finally, I was brought into a huge room lined with bookcases.

"Who are you?" Reb Layzer Gravitzer thundered, cocking his long, hairy ear.

Then he took the book, a Talmud, from the shelf and gave it to me. I said good day, but he did not respond. I wanted to leave through one door, but another door opened and in came a fat woman wearing a huge marriage wig overlaid with braids and curls and studded with little combs. A golden chain hung from her thick neck. Many rings bedecked her short fingers, and long earrings dangled from her earlobes. This was the mistress of the house, Reb Layzer Gravitzer's wife.

Just as Reb Layzer Gravitzer had to play the role of the Biblical Og, the King of Bashan, so his wife had to be the saintly woman, the kindly soul. She approached and amiably asked me who I was, pinched my cheek, and wanted to know if I was hungry. I swore I was full, but she led me into the grand salon, where perhaps twenty women, young, old, dark, blond, each one beautifully dressed and bejeweled, were sitting. The place was full of sweet fragrances and the aroma of wealth. Some women picked up a certain type of eyeglass—a lorgnette—and looked at me. Some were amazed; others smiled. The very young ones laughed.

"The Talmud folio is bigger than he is," one of them cried out.

183

They gave me a slice of sponge cake, a goblet of wine, and some brandy, which made my nose tingle and my eyes tear.

Someone asked me, "What would you like to be when you grow up, a rabbi or a teacher?"

I was already too old for such questions, so I replied, "I don't know yet."

This prompted an outburst of laughter, and they gave me some more liquor to drink. Then a woman packed some cookies and strudel in a paper bag for me to take home, as if I were a beggar.

Reb Layzer Gravitzer's wish prevailed: he was never sent to jail. He suffered a stroke of apoplexy and died immediately. He had a big funeral where, it was reported, some people cursed him vehemently. Nevertheless, he was buried in the choicest of graves, in the very first row, and a rabbi delivered the eulogy.

After his death his creditors descended on his apartment like locusts. But everything had already been inventoried. The landlord finally evicted the family from the apartment and their furniture was auctioned off. Of all his possessions only the bedding remained.

I don't know what became of Reb Layzer Gravitzer's family, but I would occasionally see Dovidl on the street carrying his violin. He wore his hair long under a broad hat. People had predicted that Dovidl would become a great violinist, but as far as I know, no one in the musical world has heard of him. Along with Reb Layzer Gravitzer everything fell apart.

My father would say to me, "What a shame! Had he put his sharp mind into studying, he would have become a brilliant Jewish scholar."

REB YEKL SAFIR

ॐ

On Gnoyna Street lived a jeweler named Reb Yekl Safir who was both a scholar and a rich man. Reb Yekl Safir was sickly and had a consumptive pallor. He had a pitch-black beard, a beaked nose, and a pair of deep black eyes which seemed to express the sadness of the world. Reb Yekl's tragedy was that he had no children. His wife, Zeldele, would always say that God had shut her womb and that there would be no one to say Kaddish for her. The couple had a housemaid named Shifra whom they treated like a daughter, but that did not suffice.

Reb Yekl Safir supported young men who studied Torah. Most of his energies were devoted to the students in the "collective" on Shliske Street. He called them his children and complained about them as if they were his own. My brother Israel Joshua had once studied in that collective and Reb Yekl Safir liked him. He loved bemoaning the fact that he had been wronged by those whom he was helping. Occasionally, he would come to visit us and I heard him complaining to my brother.

"When this fellow came to Warsaw he wore tattered rags. I clothed him as if he were my own son. I bought him everything: shirts, underwear, socks. He spent days and nights in my house. Now that he's made an excellent match, he didn't even invite me to the engagement party . . . So look, I ask you: does it pay to do favors? Zeldele was crying all night long. She swore she wouldn't let another student cross her threshold. Is there any justice?"

"There is no justice."

"What? Really? . . . After all, there has to be some order in this world . . . Hanukkah is coming and I want to have a feast— but how can I talk to Zeldele about feasts if her heart is bitter?"

Reb Yekl Safir was always hosting little feasts. As sad as he was, he longed only for joy. My brother would occasionally take me along to his apartment. I remember best a feast for the students on Shushan Purim, the day after Purim. The students drank wine, beer, and mead in a living room that had three windows; they cracked nuts and ate babkas baked by Zeldele and Shifra the maid. My brother, in disguise, pretended to be a woman who comes to ask a rabbi a question and then a couple asking for a divorce. He had the ability to change his voice, to lower it to a bass, and then switch to a screeching soprano. He improvised the lines, which were very witty, and his sketches made everyone laugh. Reb Yekl Safir laughed so much tears ran down into his black beard. Zeldele and Shifra laughed so hard they fell into each other's arms. Then the boys danced in a circle and made Reb Yekl Safir join in. I, a little boy, hopped in the middle.

Later Zeldele and Shifra brought more refreshments and Yekl Safir declared, "Children, what do I want? Just to forget my melancholy for a little while. If I hadn't been a dry tree, I would have had grandchildren by now. But I am all alone. If not for you, a holiday would have no meaning whatsoever."

Then Zeldele broke in: "But they'll scatter like swallows. As soon as they get engaged they'll forget all about us. They'll run off without even inviting us to their weddings."

"Let them run. I'm not stopping them. But now it's a holiday. If they want to be cruel ingrates, let them be cruel ingrates . . . I, Yekl Safir, have broad shoulders . . . God has punished us . . . Well, are natural children any better? They get married and forget their parents . . . And what about our Shifra? As soon as she gets married, she'll thumb her nose at us, too."

"The old man shouldn't talk that way. I'm going to be better than a daughter."

"We'll see, we'll see. People are false. I've been fooled more times than I have hairs on my head. But when I see a young scholar suffering, I must help him. I'll gladly give him the shirt off my back."

"You're a fool, my husband, a fool."

"And you're smart, Zeldele? When the fellows don't come, you badger me."

While husband and wife bandied words, the students ate, sang, cracked jokes, and planned new feasts which Yekl Safir would underwrite. My brother was one of the few students with whom Yekl Safir felt entirely comfortable, and he loved him like a son.

On the day my parents and sister left for the wedding in Berlin, my brother planned a feast for his fellow students in our house. This was the first time Reb Yekl Safir was an invited guest instead of a host. He came with his wife and their maid, Shifra. Women neighbors cooked the supper for the students. Girls from neighboring apartments offered to help in this unusual celebration.

Reb Yekl Safir ordered wine and beer. I don't remember what we did with our younger brother, Moishe. No doubt he slept at a neighbor's house. The students drank, laughed, joked, and danced. We danced so long that the janitor came up, yelling that the whitewashed ceiling was crumbling on the floor below. A policeman came to inquire whether we had a permit for the gathering. He threatened to press charges until Reb Yekl Safir called him into another room and slipped something into his hand. Afterward, Reb Yekl Safir, who was half drunk, began preaching.

"Fellas, you're all my children . . . You have all become embedded in my heart . . . Thousands of students have come through my house and I remember every single one . . . Some already have children and they are my grandchildren."

Reb Yekl Safir began to cry—and soon Zeldele, too, was wiping the tears from her eyes and kissing Shifra the maid.

The whole two weeks my parents were away in Berlin anarchy reigned in our apartment. Girls came in to cook and clean for us. Someone prepared the Sabbath cholent. My brother painted pictures in Father's courtroom and brought home loads of books.

I tried to read but understood very little. I was still a cheder lad, but I rarely attended. My parents needed me to help out at home. The truth was, I hated the cheder, and my family quickly got used to the fact that I attended when I wanted to and didn't when I didn't. Moreover, my father didn't have enough money to pay the teacher and I went to cheder for next to nothing. But I was a quick learner of the Five Books of Moses and of the Gemara, too.

I met a boy on Krochmalna Street who was in a similar situation. A few years older than I, he was as black as a Gypsy and his sidecurls stuck out like two hairpins. Even though he had parents, he looked ragged and tattered and straggled about like an orphan. He told me weird things: behind Warsaw there were deserts and fields which no one owned and where wild cows grazed. From time to time wild men could be seen there, too.

"If the cows are wild, can you take them home?" I asked him.

"No one knows the way."

"So how do you know about it?"

"From the Kabbalah."

Yes, this boy named Boruch Dovid persuaded me that he was a Kabbalist and that he knew the Zohar. He said he could draw wine from the wall and make pigeons appear by pronouncing the holy names of God. I asked him to teach me Kabbalah, but he said that I was still too young.

"And you're old?"

"I am a reincarnation of a saint."

We walked along the Warsaw streets, and he told me about the seven heavens, angels, seraphim, the holy beasts. But Boruch Dovid knew Warsaw even better than he knew the heavens. He brought me to an inn where provincial Jews who came to Warsaw to buy provisions parked their wagons. He showed me Warsaw's famous prison, the Paviak, and the arsenal at Dluga Street. He even knew the way to the Warsaw suburb of Praga. We walked along Senator Street and crossed the Praga bridge. He pulled a cork out of his pocket and threw it into the Vistula River.

"It's going to float all the way out to the sea," he said.

"And from there?"

"From there to the ocean."

"And from there?"

"From there it will reach the end of the world."

"And what's there?"

"That's where the darkness begins."

"And what's on the other side of the darkness?"

"One is forbidden to think about that. He who thinks about it will go mad."

We walked up to the Tereshpolye terminal to watch the trains come and go. A locomotive belched smoke and hissed; a bell rang out. A gigantic gendarme, his chest covered with medals, kept order. My sister had gone off somewhere to a strange young man. My parents were in Berlin. My brother Israel Joshua was reading heretical books, and I was standing somewhere in a distant terminal watching people depart for places hundreds of miles away. Boruch Dovid told me that this train went to Siberia, to China, even to the place where black men live.

A young man, probably a recruit, was leaving on a trip. He wore high boots and held a wooden suitcase. A girl in a short dress and a flowered scarf had come to see him off. They kissed each other again and again. He put his hands on her hips. Their mouths pressed hungrily one against the other. They did not want to let go.

Boruch Dovid wagged a finger. "They have sex."

"What does that mean?"

And then Boruch Dovid revealed the secret of intercourse. Everybody does it: people, animals, even flies.

"Rabbis, too?"

"Rabbis, too."

"And rabbinic judges?"

"Rabbinic judges, too."

"You're a liar! You're making it up!"

"I'm not a liar. I'll swear by my ritual fringes."

I wanted to spit in his face, but I needed him because I didn't know the way back home. A deep sadness came over me: I fell into a reverie. Many mysteries suddenly became clear to me. Adults only pretended to be saintly. They may speak about God, but secretly, so that the children won't find out, they do all kinds of abominable acts. Even my own parents. Even my own sister.

Boruch Dovid and I were angry at each other, but nevertheless we returned home together, walking somewhat apart. Perhaps the heretics are right, I thought. Perhaps there is no God. And perhaps nothing exists. Perhaps all of this is just a dream. Perhaps all people are demons and Boruch Dovid is a demon, too.

It was dark when I got home. I hadn't eaten all day. The door opened and Manya the neighbor's daughter came in.

"Why were you running around all day? Mama expected you for lunch."

"I'm not hungry."

"They're calling, come eat with us."

"I don't want to eat."

"Want me to bring it in here?"

I didn't reply. Manya brought me potatoes and borscht and a cutlet. She sat down opposite me and watched me eat.

"Do you miss your mommy?"

"No."

"Do you miss your daddy?"

"I don't miss anyone."

"What are you gonna be when you grow up?"

"A heretic."

"What's that mean?"

"That there's no God."

"Oh, one is forbidden to talk like that!"

"But you can."

"They'll burn you and roast you in hell!"

"I'll pour water on and douse the flames."

Manya laughed. I saw the dimples in her cheeks. She looked just like her mother, Pesele. Her two braids were tied with a red ribbon.

"Why don't you wash your face?"

"Because I'm a chimney sweep."

"Boy, are you strange!"

"I'm a robber. I have horns!"

And I put two fingers to my forehead. Manya smiled, but she was also a bit scared.

After she left, I went to bed and immediately sank into a heavy sleep. I woke up in the middle of the night. My older brother had not come home. I was all alone in the apartment. I recalled Boruch Dovid's remarks about the cork that floated all the way to the darkness at the end of the world. But how could the world have an end? There had to be something on the other side of the darkness. And what was there before the world was created? Who had created the darkness and the void? Oh, I hope I don't go mad!

I had a crazy impulse: to go out on the balcony. I opened the door and a cold wind swept over me. Krochmalna Street was empty. All the stores were shuttered. Not a soul on the square. The only sounds were the hissing of the mist-wrapped gas lanterns. A sky thickly sown with stars arched over the roofs. I suddenly felt afraid and began to cry. I was all alone in the world, surrounded by hidden monstrosities and mysteries that no one could resolve.

FATHER BECOMES AN
"ANARCHIST"

౧౦

Waiting for the Messiah was not a distant dream in our house but a daily concern. Earning money became increasingly difficult. Father was anguished that his children were straying from the right path. Warsaw was full of Zionists, strikers, and just plain Jews who cooked on the Sabbath and didn't observe the dietary laws. In Berlin Father had experienced for the first time a city where pious Jews were relegated to a tiny corner, surrounded by a goyish world. Where would all this lead? There was only one way out: the Messiah would have to come and put an end to poverty, the Exile, and heresy. Father would often speak to me about the Messiah. He reminded me of the saying that if all Jews would observe even two Sabbaths the Messiah would come. Father would repeat at every opportunity the conviction that everything depended on us Jews and that we were responsible for the anguish we suffered.

Father often returned after prayers from the Radziminer *shtibl* with all kinds of news and plans. Whenever we heard Father running up the steps of our apartment, we knew he was bringing some item of interest from the *shtibl*. Where my mother was skeptical by nature, Father was excitable and felt the need to share his enthusiasm with his family and even with strangers.

It was a summer evening. We heard Father running up the stairs, panting. He pushed open the door, his blue eyes and fiery red beard glowing with high spirits. The possibility that the Messiah had come ran through my mind.

"Good evening!"

"A good year!"

"I heard some news in the *shtibl*!" Father said. "Something extraordinary!"

"What is it? Has the Radziminer saint performed another miracle?" Mother asked mockingly.

"A new society has been founded, whose members call themselves anarchists," Father said. "They want to do away with money. Why do we need money? Money cannot be eaten. All troubles stem from money. The anarchists' plan is that every person should work four hours a day and in return should be given all his necessities. Every person will have to work. And I'm going to become a shoemaker!" Father said boldly. "I'm going to make boots four hours a day, and then I'm going to sit and study. Just as it is written: 'Love work and hate the rabbinate.'"

The idea that Father would become a shoemaker prompted laughter in the house. Father smiled, too, but he seemed thoroughly taken by this new idea. Why he called it "anarchism" and not "socialism" I do not know. Evidently that is how they sold it to him.

"Many great people have come around to this idea," Father continued, "including generals and counts. They lack nothing, but they want justice. Everything stems from work. A house is built by one person, a garment is sewn by another. To make bread someone must plow, sow, and reap. Nothing comes from money. So if that's the case, why do we need money? All week long people will work, and on Friday they'll get a receipt showing that they've worked, and on the basis of this receipt people will be able to get everything they need from the store."

I liked this idea. But my mother began to ask questions. "And what about an apartment?"

"Everybody will get an apartment."

"Who would choose an attic or a cellar? Since everyone would work four hours, everyone would want a beautiful apartment."

"People will cast lots."

"And what would happen if someone came into a store and asked for ten garments instead of one?"

"Why should he want more? Everybody would take what he needs."

"Some people live on fancy Marshalkovska Street," Mother said, "while others live somewhere in the back of the city, on the outskirts of town, in Peltzovizna, or even in Siberia. If everyone is equal, everyone would want to live on Marshalkovska Street."

"What does it matter where you live?"

"Everyone would want the best and the most beautiful for himself."

"That's only because of money. Once the evil impulse for money disappears, people will be satisfied with a little bit," Father said.

"If everybody works, whom will a person go to for religious questions?" I asked.

"I will decide religious questions," Father replied, "but without charge. One is forbidden to take money for deciding religious questions or judging a lawsuit. One is not allowed to use one's Torah learning as a source of income."

"And what will they do with money?"

"Paper money is just paper, it has no value. From the gold they'll make jewelry, or who knows what."

Father spoke of all this as if it would happen soon, tomorrow, but Mother gave the wise smile of a knowing adult who is listening to childish fantasies.

"Go wash. Supper's getting cold!"

At the meal Father didn't stop speaking about anarchism.

"Of course Jews long for the Messiah, but while we're in Exile it would be quite a good thing. We wouldn't have to pay rent. There would be no thieves. Why would a thief steal if he could work four hours a day? We wouldn't need policemen or janitors to lock the gates, and there wouldn't be any soldiers or wars. Because why do kings wage wars? For money."

"Father, would the Czar have to work also?"

"Why not? Every king would have to learn a trade," Father said. "Our Czar would learn shoemaking. A king would have to learn a trade. Otherwise what would he do when he's no longer the king? He'd have to go begging from door to door. But with a trade his livelihood would be secure."

"And who would remove the garbage?" Mother asked. "And who would want to be a tanner? And who would want to be a chimney sweep and risk his life crawling on roofs?"

Father's explanations were in vain. Mother's questions grew sharper and sharper. Suddenly Mother declared, "And why should the rich agree to this? They have palaces, maids, servants, coaches. Why should Rothschild give away all that he has and learn how to become a shoemaker?"

"So that justice would prevail. Generals and counts have joined this movement."

"Perhaps one crazy general did. The rich don't need justice. The peasants starve while the rich send their darling sons to Paris to carouse. Why would they want to become equal with peasants?"

Father gave all kinds of answers, but the notion that the rich could simply be forced did not occur to him. "Force" and "might" were words that my father never considered. The core of all his remarks was that once everyone understood the benefits, all would agree.

Father finished supper quicker than usual and asked for the fingerbowl to dip his fingers before saying grace. He rarely spent time on the balcony, but that night he asked me to bring a chair out for him. I took one for myself as well. Outside it was hot, noisy, full of chimney smoke. Father sat and described the anarchists' plans to me. Everyone would work and everyone would have an income. At age thirteen every boy would learn a trade. No line of work would be disgraceful. Nowadays people are ashamed of a trade because a worker is poor and also because workers are considered common. They have no time to study, but with a four-hour day everyone would be a scholar. In the Talmud we learn about the sages Rabbi Yochanan the shoemaker and Rabbi Joshua the blacksmith. In ancient times it wasn't shameful to be a laborer. Our forefather Jacob was a shepherd, and so were Moses and King David.

"Father, what will I be?"

"You're also going to be a shoemaker. We'll work together. And after work we'll sit and study."

"Where will we work?"

"At home."

"In the living room?"

"Why not?"

"Father, you can't be a shoemaker."

"Why not? It's an easy line of work."

I always loved my father but that evening I loved him even more. Of all the news that he brought from the *shtibl* I liked this item best. I kissed him and combed his beard with my fingers. Father sat on the balcony until late at night, depicting the happy times to come, when there would be no need for money and everyone would work and study Torah. Then he began reciting the bedtime prayer "Hear O Israel." I hoped that this plan would quickly come true. I could already see my father sitting at a cobbler's bench holding a hammer, an awl, and shoemaker's thread, and me sitting next to him. People still come to us with lawsuits, but they don't pay for the service. I go to Esther's candy store and they give me everything free: chocolate, ice cream, cookies, caramels.

However, days passed and we did not hear anything about anarchism. Every time Father returned from the Radziminer *shtibl*, I asked him what was happening with the anarchists. Each time he replied, "Things like that don't happen overnight."

"How long will it take?"

"A while."

I realized then that Father's enthusiasm for the matter had cooled considerably. Apparently someone in the Radziminer *shtibl* had told him that this entire philosophy was incompatible with Judaism. He no longer wanted to discuss it. When I asked him, he responded, "Be a Jew and the Messiah will come."

The Messiah had to come, because our poverty at home was worsening. All kinds of troubles beset us. My sister in Antwerp sent us a depressing eight-page letter. The paper was tear-stained. She had already given birth to a boy, Moishele. But there was a crisis among the diamond cutters and polishers. Her husband had been out of work for weeks and months. Other young people took on different jobs, but her husband knew no other line of work. He hadn't brought home a franc, and she and her child were in dire straits.

As poor as we were, we had to send money to Belgium. There were very few lawsuits, and when somebody did come for one, Father would be in the Hasidic *shtibl* or at the ritual bath. I would go to call him, but the litigants rarely wanted to wait.

I remember one such incident very well. Just after Father left the house to go to the ritual bath on Gnoyna Street, some people came who were willing to wait for Father. I ran to the ritual bath, but getting there was tricky. One had to go down a staircase and pass all kinds of apartments with half-painted walls and protruding pipes in which either hot water or steam flowed. This wasn't just a ritual bath but an entire labyrinth.

I stumbled about lost, as if in a dream. I opened one door and saw a naked woman who started screaming. I got scared, worrying that I wouldn't make it out of all these corridors and passageways alive. Finally, I found the men's ritual bath. Father was not there. Men walked about naked. How weird they looked with their wet beards, dripping sidecurls, and hairy and sagging limbs. And they were bareheaded to boot. Only one man stood in the water, and all the others looked at him in astonishment, wagging their fingers at him. The water was boiling hot. No one else dared set foot in it. But this one man with a black beard and bright red skin was soaking in it. Every once in a while he dunked his head; when he surfaced he cried out breathlessly, "Oh, it's delicious! May no goy ever feel how good it is!"

I returned home and saw that the men were no longer there—they couldn't wait any longer.

"Did you find him, that insufferable shlimazel?" Mother said. Both she and I knew that one was forbidden to speak that way about Father. But our poverty was oppressive. We were supposed to have paid twenty-four rubles in rent on the eighth of the month. But now the eighth was coming again and we still hadn't paid. Reb Mendl, the landlord, always sent the janitor to demand payment. He threatened to inventory our belongings and put them up for public auction. We owed money in every shop. We looked bedraggled and couldn't afford to buy new clothes. Mother said bitterly, "Where did he disappear to? Among normal people the man of the house thinks of livelihood, but *he* spends days on end in the study houses. What's going to become of us?"

And then out of the blue she remarked, "Ah, woe, I've been asked to divorce him!"

The idea that my parents might get divorced and become strangers was unimaginably horrible. It was almost as wild as the fact that my parents had once been strangers and a matchmaker had brought them together. Our world was full of awful truths. The older I got, the more these truths tore open my eyes, increasing the turmoil that encompassed me.

MY FATHER'S FRIEND

I often hear Yiddish writers talking about publishing and distributing books. They'll speak of typesetting, matrices, plates, sheets of paper. But I'm probably one of the few writers who have known the terminology of printing from very early childhood. My father wrote commentaries on sacred texts and had his books printed. Early on, I knew about typesetting a book with lead font, correcting galleys, handling matrices, pouring lead, printing, and binding. Despite my father's meager income, he saved money in order to publish his books. Father would say, "A book remains forever."

Aside from publishing his own books, he also edited a manuscript by Rabbi Joseph Shor, author of *Pri Megadim*. I remember that manuscript as if it were before me. It was bound and had faded letters on yellowish-gray paper. Nevertheless, the handwriting, which even then was one hundred and fifty years old, was still legible. The title of the book was *Notrikon*, and like everything else that Rabbi Joseph Shor had written, its style was obtuse. Father worked on this old manuscript with a good friend, known in rabbinic circles for his books and whom I will call Reb Nachman.

It was a great joy for me to stand by the table and listen to Father talking with Reb Nachman. Both had reddish beards and blue eyes, but Reb Nachman was an elegant Hasid. His alpaca gaberdine always sparkled. On his nose rested a pair of gold-rimmed glasses, which hung on a black string. His boots were polished to a bright shine. Smart and gentle, he came from a fine family and was a former student of Reb Tzodik Lubliner, who during his lifetime had written several hundred books, which Reb Nachman kept reprinting. Father enjoyed Reb Nachman's bon mots, and Reb Nachman enjoyed Father's bold talk. They hit it off very well. Although I heard Reb Nachman call the Radziminer Rebbe by some nasty names, Reb Nachman's entire behavior was that of a scholar and an aristocrat.

But woe unto Jewish aristocrats!

For despite all the books that Reb Nachman published, he didn't earn a penny from them—and so his son had to make cigarettes. Apparently this was not a kosher line of work. It was contraband, because packs of cigarettes were supposed to bear a customs tax stamp proving that the duty had been paid. But, after all, what could a scholarly Jew with a wife and children do? His son peddled these cigarettes to stores, and this was a supplement to their earnings, perhaps their sole income.

One day my father sent me to Reb Nachman's house, but I don't remember why. His apartment was somewhat different from ours. They had more children and also more furniture. He sat at his desk wearing an old vest and a little cap. Spread out before him were colored slate pencils and bottles of ink and India ink. Reb Nachman not only had a beautiful handwriting

but, with the talent of a graphic artist, he could also "print" letters to decorate title pages with all kinds of little flowers,
wheels, and circles.

Since Reb Nachman often came to us and my father rarely
went to visit him, I was given a royal welcome. Reb Nachman
talked to me as if I were his equal. Since he had already heard
that my older brother, Israel Joshua, had strayed from the path,
he spoke to me about the heretics. He showed me a sheet of
paper on which he had drawn all manner of flowers, small birds,
and eagles.

"Have a look," he said. "If somebody told you that all this
came about of its own accord, you'd say that man is crazy. But
the heretics say that the world was created by itself. Isn't that
madness?"

"Yes, of course."

"And man, they say, is descended from monkeys. But where
did the monkey come from? Can a monkey create itself?"

"No."

"And the earth, they say, was torn from the sun. Well then,
where did the sun come from? They'll babble all kinds of nonsense as long as they don't have to admit the truth that there is
a Creator."

Reb Nachman's remarks made me blush. In our house I
wasn't spoken to with such respect. There I was just a little boy.
But here they treated me like a young man and served me a
glass of tea and a cookie. A girl my age with dark hair and long
braids came into the room, followed by another girl. I could
smell cutlets frying in the kitchen. Reb Nachman's apartment
was not as bare as ours. Here everything mingled: Torah, clever
talk, girls, good cooking, and a table full of pencils, inks, brushes,

and stencils. Reb Nachman even discussed the heretics, whose views I had wanted to know for a long time.

Then I heard loud banging on the front door. There was an uproar; gentiles were talking. Reb Nachman jumped up from his chair. I too stood and witnessed a bizarre scene: the kitchen was full of police. I saw a detective, an investigating officer, and other officials with gilt-button uniforms bedecked with little crowns. The janitor followed them, hat in hand. Even a man dressed in civilian clothes came with them, a secret agent. I didn't understand their Russian, but from the way the officials yelled, stomped their boots, and held their swords, I realized that this was an inspection. Reb Nachman's face turned as white as paper. The frightened little girls shrank into a corner. His wife pleaded with the men, but they shouted at her. I was very frightened and began to tremble.

"Can I go home?" I asked Reb Nachman.

He looked at me in confusion. "If they let you."

I moved toward the door, but a policeman stopped me. "Where are you going?"

I either didn't know about Reb Nachman's business or didn't know that he dealt in illicit goods. I stood there shaking. A while back, my friend Boruch Dovid and I had seen the Warsaw prison, its yellow walls, barred windows covered with iron mesh netting, behind which stood sallow-faced prisoners, and the black gates through which the prisoners were brought in police wagons.

I was certain that my time had come and I would be put in jail. I would rot there between the thick walls along with Reb Nachman and his family and no one would come to save me. But why did I deserve this? And what did they want from Reb

Nachman and his little girls? Was he the victim of a false accusation? Had a decree been issued against him?

I recalled the story of Rabbi Akiva, who had been tortured with iron combs and whose soul departed with the words "Hear O Israel." Would I come to a similar end? Had the Khmelnitski period returned, or the era of the destruction of the Holy Temple?

Oh, if only I could jump out the window! Oh, if only I could suddenly sprout wings and fly off like an eagle! Oh, if I could suddenly become as strong as the mighty Samson and grab a jawbone and begin beating these Philistines! Or if I had the sort of hat that could make me invisible, I'd walk out the door and they'd see only emptiness.

I hadn't yet been arrested, but such a strong desire to be free came over me that I thought, What have I lacked till now? What was there to worry about when I could walk down the streets freely? The summer day, the Warsaw streets, our own home suddenly became dear and precious to me. I looked fearfully at the swords, the epaulets, the whistles, the medals. A thought ran through my head: If there was a God, why was He silent? How could He permit such wicked men to torment Jews?

After some discussion the policemen began searching the apartment. One remained standing by the door. At first they found nothing; then suddenly from somewhere they began pulling out boxes of cigarettes and cigarette paper, tobacco, and, I think, other merchandise as well, wrapped in all kinds of paper and tissue paper. And if that wasn't enough, the civilian brought a crowbar and they started breaking open the floorboards. They opened the floor at the proper spot, under which they found more boxes and paper-wrapped goods.

"Someone informed on us!" Reb Nachman exclaimed.

"Be quiet! No talking!" ordered a policeman.

The inspection lasted about three hours. Perspiration poured out of me and I nearly melted. It threaded down my back, over my belly, over my entire body. My shirt was soaking wet. Even the policemen noticed and joked about it. One of them grabbed one of my sidecurls, but his hand got wet. I felt myself being overwhelmed by fear. I felt everything in me melting away; soon, I thought, there'd be nothing left.

Reb Nachman's girls looked at me, and even though the family was in trouble, they smiled. After a while, it appeared that all the perspiration had run out of me. But I still stood there trembling and quaking with fear and shame. These gentiles, with their swords, revolvers, Russian talk, peasant jokes, awoke in me a hatred that I had never before felt toward any other person. I stood face-to-face with the evil ones.

I don't recall exactly how it ended, but when Reb Nachman's son finally arrived, he took some of the officials into a bedroom, spoke confidentially, and made a deal with them. All my fear had been in vain. Neither he nor any other member of his household was dragged off to jail.

After the policemen left, Reb Nachman took hold of his beard and said, "What a life for Jews! I swear, it's high time for the Messiah to come."

They wanted to give me some more snacks and invited me to stay for a meal, but I wanted to leave this apartment. What had happened here not only frightened me but troubled me greatly. I had already heard plenty of my brother's complaints that Jews were little shopkeepers, business agents, idlers, and nondescripts. There were more shopkeepers than customers. Fathers-in-law gave their sons-in-law free board for several years, but they themselves had nothing to eat. My brother spoke of the Land of Israel, where Jews had taken up farming and were becoming a normal people. He also insinuated that those who toiled bitterly had nothing to eat for the Sabbath, while those who walked about with nothing to do were loaded with gold. He had spoken with Mother about the Bilgoray sievemakers, who slaved away in the workshops all week long and on Fridays went begging from door to door.

"Why don't they strike?" my brother asked. "The owners would have to submit."

Mother, too, had begun using weird words ever since she'd returned from Berlin, where my sister's wedding had taken place.

"In Germany people are free," Mother said. "The policemen speak politely with people and say 'please' and 'excuse me' . . . At the border they didn't rummage through our suitcases and they called Father 'Herr Rabbiner' . . ."

All this talk spun in my head and formed a knot. I wandered the streets, and something seethed and boiled in me. My brother's words awakened a feeling in me which mingled with my own thoughts. No, this was no way to live. Life here was one big disgrace, absolutely disgusting!

For the first time I began to look at the Jews of Warsaw with a new set of eyes. I saw tiny shops, tattered people, dirty, bedraggled children, disheveled women. From the study houses and *shtibls* the voice of the Torah was heard, but surrounding all this were Poles, peasants, and countless goyim who hated Jews and considered them freeloaders, beggars, parasites. The Jews had only one protector: God in heaven. But what if, God forbid, the heretics were right?

A FORGED IOU

ॐ

This story must be told. It is a testament to human innocence and human wickedness.

One day a Russian document was delivered to our house. It wasn't carried by the mailman but by a court clerk. Since my father could not read Russian, we called in a neighbor who had been in the army. The man read, shrugged his shoulders, and told my father that he was being ordered to pay six hundred rubles for an IOU he had endorsed. My father stood there astounded. In his entire life he had never signed an IOU nor had he ever endorsed one.

"It must be a mistake!" he said.

But apparently it was not a mistake. The promissory note had my father's exact name: Pinchos Menachem Mendl, and also his family name and exact address. The document demanded that my father pay his debt at once and warned him that if he did not pay, his furniture would be inventoried and auctioned off publicly.

In short, it turned out that someone had forged my father's signature. My father was terror-stricken. He had a typically

Jewish, scholarly repugnance for anything having to do with police, gentiles, courts of law, and their entire legal system. Merely looking at a sword, epaulets, and the gilt buttons of a uniform frightened my father. From his reading he knew that the masters of this world were all evil, knew nothing of justice, and always sided with the strong and the false. Woe unto those who had any dealings with the police authorities! No one escaped from their hands in one piece.

Mother and we children tried to console Father. After all, this was not a criminal proceeding. Second, the matter could easily be proved in court. Experts could be called in. But these words alone—criminal proceedings, court, experts!—cast an extraordinary pall of fear over Father. All he wanted to do was pray, study, and immerse himself in Yiddishkeit—and now he would have to find a lawyer. Who knows, perhaps they would even ask him to swear in court? Who knows whether he might have to stand among these uncircumcised ones bareheaded? Furthermore, the lawyer would have to be paid and there wasn't a penny in the house.

Father finally found a small-time lawyer who discovered that the IOU had been presented and forged by a merchant named Lula. My father went to see him. Lula had a cotton-and-accessories shop and wore Western-style garb.

Father confronted him: "What do you want from me? I'm a poor man. Where am I supposed to get six hundred rubles from?"

Lula looked frightened at first, because the punishment for forging an IOU was three years in jail. But when he saw that my father was pleading with him, he understood that a naïve, innocent man was standing before him and he said, "Rabbi, you better pay up! If not, I'll let them put you into jail."

"Wait a minute! I didn't sign this IOU. I don't even know you. This entire thing is a false accusation."

"You *did* sign it!"

"When? How?"

"I don't have time to argue with you. Pay up! You're a man with a beard and sidecurls, but you don't want to pay. You're a thief!"

And that is how Lula, that brazen lout, spoke to my father.

The signature was written in Latin characters, in Polish, and my father knew how to sign his name only in Russian, which used the Cyrillic alphabet. But Lula did not know this. He had already exchanged the promissory note for merchandise or for other expenses, and either could not or did not want to redeem the note. He had decided to let the matter take its course. Meanwhile, he was free of the obligation to pay.

My father went about worried and pale. He could no longer study in peace or pray with devotion. The small-time lawyer wasn't suitable for such a complicated lawsuit and my father went to see Noah Prilutsky, the famous philologist, the son of Zvi Prilutsky, the editor of the Yiddish newspaper *The Moment.* No sooner had my father uttered two words than Prilutsky exclaimed, "You're from the Lublin district."

"Yes, how did you know?"

"From the way you speak. Didn't you once live in Tomashov?"

"Yes, I am from Tomashov."

Father told Prilutsky his story, and Prilutsky laughed. "Don't worry, Rabbi, you won't pay an IOU that you didn't sign. Let the other fellow, the forger, that swindler, worry."

Prilutsky promised Father he'd call Lula and talk severely with him. But in the meantime Prilutsky had to travel somewhere and could not undertake the case.

That promissory note was in the hands of a gentile firm, and since Lula had signed over his store and all his valuables to his wife's name, the firm hired a lawyer who demanded payment from Father. The lawyer knew quite well that Father was innocent. But the difference between a criminal and a lawyer is often a tiny one. The other lawyer abused my father and said that it was a shame that a rabbi, a man of the spirit, should refuse to pay a sum of money which he had guaranteed.

For the first time in his life Father was face-to-face with a world where people thought one thing and said another. They knew the truth—but they concocted false accusations. Father was beside himself.

"Ah, woe, how can this be?" he said. "We are in Sodom! This is exactly like the Beilis trial!"

Father predicted a bitter turn of events: they would take everything from him, God forbid, and put him in jail. He would not be able to pray, study, or write commentaries. He would be forced to eat nonkosher food and be sent in chains to Siberia. If they could dream up such lies and tell him to his face that he had signed an IOU that he did not sign, then it was the end of the world! Then we were back in the generation of the Flood, and such liars and destroyers would not stop at any transgression. Hadn't the informer Avigdor been responsible for the imprisonment of the holy Rabbi Shneur Zalman of Lyady? And hadn't the revered Rabbi Meir of Rothenberg also been put in jail?

Father turned to holy texts that discussed martyrdom. He began repenting and fasting. If such a calamity was destined for him, it was a sign that he deserved it. It was summer and Lula had gone off on vacation. The new lawyer whom Father had engaged traveled to a spa. A trial date had been set, but it was postponed. The judge and the experts were hunting beasts somewhere in the forest; that the rabbi from Krochmalna Street couldn't sleep at night was no concern of theirs.

In the Radziminer *shtibl,* men who had some experience rebuked Father for being afraid. One Hasid even regretted that this hadn't happened to him. He would have gotten lots of money out of Lula; if not, he would have Lula put in jail. Some of the wealthy Jews in the *shtibl* laughed into their fists.

"What will they be able to take from you?" they asked. "Your *Yoreh De'ah* or your Talmud? Lula is probably waiting until after the holidays, when people start buying cotton. Then he'll pay up."

Everyone had a different opinion, but Father went about deep in thought. He knew that there were demons, imps, ghosts, spirits, unclean people who did evil deeds. But this was the first time that Satan had latched on to him and tried to destroy him. What bothered Father most of all was Lula's impudence. How could someone lie so brazenly to another person's face? He's a Jew, after all. He speaks Yiddish. From whom did such a sinner of Israel stem? Where did he get such cruelty? How could he sit there on vacation among the trees, breathing fresh air and eating, when he had sucked the blood out of a fellow Jew? And if a Jew could perpetrate such an injustice, how could we complain about goyish behavior?

"Ah woe, it's not good. It's as bitter as gall." Father could not stop sighing. "No doubt, these are Messianic times."

My brother, who had begun to stray from the Jewish path, offered arguments that supported his own point of view. "Since Jews are the chosen people, the ones who say in prayers 'You have chosen us,' how can a person like Lula be among them?"

"When a Jew abandons the Torah, he's worse than a goy," Father replied.

"But there are also bankrupts among the Hasidim," my brother argued. "You, Father, don't know what's happening in the Nalevke district or in Lodz. Every other merchant declares bankruptcy. They sign IOUs and then they put off payment until they declare bankruptcy. Then they settle for thirty kopecks on the ruble and can once again continue doing business. And these very same Jews come to see the Rebbe of Gur! The rebbe himself is a partner in a lottery, and he himself has declared bankruptcy."

"Scoundrel!" Father yelled.

"I'm telling the truth."

"A swindler is not a Hasid, and a Hasid is not a swindler— he just calls himself a Hasid. So what can one do? If you want, you can call yourself 'governor.' We have only this Torah. We have nothing else but this Torah. It gives us life. Whoever does not believe in it is a sinner of Israel."

"Oh, Father, you don't know the world at all."

"Who makes up this world? Jews who serve the Almighty."

"It's a world full of fighting and grabbing, murder and exploitation, swindle and lies."

"That's not the world. Those are the evil ones."

"Then according to you, Father, it looks like three-quarters of the world will fry in hell."

"Hell is big enough!"

Gradually, Father recovered. If it was the will of heaven that he, Pinchos Menachem Mendl, the son of Samuel the Kohen, rot in jail, then it was probably a just decree. He surely deserved everything. The Master of the Universe was a merciful and gracious God. Nothing evil stems from Him. It is all our fault.

Rosh Hashanah came, followed by Yom Kippur and Sukkos. Father observed all the commandments connected with the Days of Awe with passionate devotion. One *mitzvah* followed another. Once again some pews were knocked together and Asher from the dairy store led the Kol Nidrei service and the Musaf service the following day.

Right after Yom Kippur Father took me to the market on Gzhibov Street to buy an *esrog*. I had a yearning for a beautiful *esrog*, but the nice ones with tiny bumps cost ten, fifteen, and twenty-five rubles. Father looked and chose one. It was a *mitzvah* to buy a beautiful *esrog*, but *mitzvah*s like that cost money. He bought a pockmarked *esrog*, scattered with tiny spots, but in compensation the *lulav* was a beauty, with myrtle and willow twigs held together with little straw rings, all placed in a nice little straw basket.

I see Father now as he walks along Gnoyna Street, the paper box containing the *esrog* wrapped in flax in one hand, and the *lulav* in the other. In the light of the sun his beard turns fiery gold. The street bustles. Women hawk their wares: grapes, plums, apples, pears, all kinds of cakes and greens. I stop.

"Father, I'd like to ask you something."

"Well, ask."

"Are all Jews' sins forgiven on Yom Kippur?"

"If one repents, the Almighty forgives."

"Was Lula also forgiven for his sin?"

Father gets confused. He looks at me askance. "It's the Eve of Sukkos. Let's not talk about this."

People are building sukkos in our courtyard. Those who can't hold a hammer are busy with boards, doors, nails. Father approaches and wants to help, too. He also wants the *mitzvah* of helping build a sukka.

The trial took place during winter, and the experts concluded that the signature was forged. Father was absolved.

The lawyer then had to draw up a complaint against Lula, the forger, who could have been given a three-year prison sentence.

Lula came running to Father. "Rabbi, do you want to kill me?"

"Why did you do such a thing to me?"

"Rabbi, I was in trouble."

"And when one is in trouble, does one forge another person's signature?"

"When one is drowning, one wants to save oneself."

He stood there in our apartment with his fat neck, pointy belly, and fashionable clothes. He even had a ring on his finger. He looked tanned and stuffed. He raged against Father, moralizing, "Rabbi, your lawyer doesn't have a Jewish heart . . . If you do such a thing, Rabbi, they'll write you up in all the news-papers . . . You won't be able to set foot outdoors . . . It's going to be a desecration of God's name!"

But Father told him forthrightly that he hadn't intended to bring a complaint against him. He would not, God forbid, send a Jew to jail.

Lula began adjusting the cuffs of his shirt. He soon took an aggressive stance.

"Just remember what you said, Rabbi! I'm not going to have anything to do with your lawyers, those rotten scoundrels . . . It all depends on you . . . Without you those lowdown skunks won't be able to do anything!"

Lula left, slamming the door behind him. It was absolutely beneath the dignity of this Mr. Lula to come to the rabbi of little Krochmalna Street. He ran down the steps. Outside, he jumped into a droshky. Father stood there for a while bemused before returning to his Talmud.

When Mother came into the room, he said, "In *shul*, I'll have to recite the blessing thanking God for saving me."